Guide to Successful

Commercial

Photography

Published by the British Journal of Photography

© 1994 Timothy Benn Publishing Ltd

Timothy
Benn
Publishing

Published by the British Journal of
Photography, 186-187 Temple Chambers,
Temple Chambers, Temple Avenue, London
EC4Y 0DB, with the support of Fuji Photo Film
(UK) Ltd, Fuji Film House, 125 Finchley Road,
London NW3 6JH

Author: Christopher Wordsworth

Editor & art direction: Chris Dickie

Illustration & design: David Livingston
& Tony Paull

Cover photographs © Sanders Nicolson,
Carl Lyttle & Ian McKinnell

Many thanks to all the photographers and
agencies without whose help and cooperation
this book would not have been posibble,
namely: Ace Photo Agency; Grahame Austin;
Martin Beckett; Steve Bicknell; Norman Childs;
Ian Coates; Peter Dazeley; Mike Hemsley;
Christopher Joyce; Jon Lippet; Jean Lock;
Peter Lowry; Carl Lyttle; Tom Mackie;
Danny Maddocks; Ian McKinnell;
Julian Nieman; Sanders Nicolson; Paul Proctor;
Bill Prudom; Michael St Maur Sheil;
Tessa Traeger; and Paul Webster. All
photographs © the photographers; all
illustrations, except where otherwise credited,
© Timothy Benn Publishing Ltd

Page makeup in Quark XPress®
Illustration in Adobe Illustrator®

First published 1994

ISBN 0 900414 47 2

In the same series: *The Fuji Manual of Wedding
& Portrait Photography*

Scanning and film output by Primary Colours,
Chiswick, Middlesex, England. Printed by
Midas Printing, Hong Kong

Photography – and its commercial realities

The assignments faced by commercial photographers, stretching both their creativity and technical skills, are arguably the most challenging in our profession.

Their product requirements in terms of quality and consistency are very exacting and it has been in listening to what advertising and industrial photographers want that we have been able to develop films such as Fujichrome Velvia, the new range of Fujichrome Provia and Fuji FP-100C instant film, which meet specific requirements in a field which demands accuracy, sharpness and performance every time.

Yet it has also been our policy to give as much help as possible to up-and-coming commercial photographers, not just to support successful professionals. That's where this book will provide, I trust, immeasurable help right where it is needed in a sophisticated and essential discipline.

In many ways, this book has evolved in a similar way to our products for professionals: many photographers have asked Fuji Professional – and of course the publishers of the *British Journal of Photography* – to produce a practical and informative guide to commercial photographic techniques and materials. We took these requests on board, and the result is the second book in the series, having produced *Wedding & Portrait Photography* in 1992.

It is our objective to help commercial photographers, assistants, students and those who have just started out by discussing the work and techniques of established photographers and showing the best examples of their work. Furthermore, we present in this book the range of products, particularly colour reversal films, which we have painstakingly developed for the commercial photographic market over the past decade.

Finally, I would like to thank those involved in commercial photography who have helped us with this book: the author, Chris Wordsworth, all the featured photographers and all those involved in its production. I hope you enjoy reading it and that you and your business benefit from it.

Graham Rutherford
Divisional Manager
Professional Photographic Division
Fuji Photo Film (UK)

• An illustration, by photographer STEVE BICKNELL, of how to turn in an attractive image even when faced with the most mundane subject matter. This is from a company profile Bicknell shot for Jaguar Business systems – further details, page 61

Business Basics
Assignments
Product photography
Industrial &
Corporate
Architecture
People
Advertising
Stock Photography
Digital Photography
Materials
Processing

Contents

Business

Commercial photography is about selling: selling products, selling ideas, selling your work. But first you need to establish what it is you have to sell. Where do your talents lie? And just as importantly, is there a place in the market for the work you produce? Once you've taken stock, you can concentrate on reaching clients, building relationships and developing your business. Whatever strategies you adopt, the business of survival in photography is a continual process. You need to stay sharp...

Measuring up

No amount of talent will guarantee success as a commercial photographer. From the outset, you must stand back from what you are doing and consider: What kind of service am I providing – and is there a demand for it?

▶ **Windowlight gives a soft, intimate feel to this lingerie shot by SANDERS NICOLSON. Although Sanders has been a 'name photographer' in the advertising business for many years, he still works hard at maintaining an edge over competitors. His portfolios, for example, are composed entirely of colour laserprints of his work (produced on a Canon CLC copier). This gives a more 'graphic' feeling to the work, and printing the pictures on flexible paper brings them closer to the finished result in a magazine or brochure. It also sets his books apart from conventional portfolios of mounted transparencies or laminated prints. All the Sanders Nicolson pictures in this book were scanned from laserprint originals.**

This book is about the business of commercial photography. We shall be meeting many highly skilled, successful photographers and finding out how they achieve stunning results. But remember, photography can be such an exciting, creatively rewarding activity, that even the most talented can sometimes forget about the commercial realities. So let's not lose sight of that word 'business'.

From time to time, it will pay you to stand back and think about your own business. Basically, it's a simple transaction: you provide a service or product – your photography – to someone who is prepared to pay you for it. In commercial terms, photography is no different to brick laying or selling cars. So let's think about the two basic elements in that formula: the product – what sort of photography you produce – and the client – the person who has a need for your type of work. Later we shall look at ways of joining the two in a mutually successful relationship: a process sometimes called 'marketing'.

Most of us got into photography because we enjoyed it. But how many of us still do the type

of photography we used to enjoy most? Any commercial career is a process of modifying what we like doing and reshaping it to what clients want to buy. But, nevertheless, photographic styles are still a very personal matter, and this can make it very difficult for photographers to make meaningful assessments of their own work.

Imagine you are buying a car. As a customer you are faced with a wide variety of choice. You also have your own requirements to help narrow down that choice: size, performance, style, price, running costs, 'image' and so on – even whether or not you trust the salesman! Your clients view you and your work in rather the same way (though they probably know somewhat less about photography than you know about cars). Because they didn't take the pictures – or spend years learning the ropes – they don't have the same emotional commitment. To them, photography is just another service they need to buy: a product which has to do a job.

So ask yourself, what sort of product do you offer? And is there sufficient demand for it? Commercial photography feeds off the needs

often more important than outstanding photography.

But let's not get too carried away with all this quality and enthusiasm. Remember, commercial photography is a business. We also need to consider costs and profitability. Many articles on business in photography stress costs above all else: majoring on accounting, overheads, business plans, taxation and so on. This is perhaps a good antidote for the tendency of photographers to overlook such matters, but on the contrary, we believe that commercial photography should be sales-lead. After all, if your work doesn't sell, you don't have a business.

Having said that, a business will also die if it doesn't make enough profit. So the third question to ask about your products is, are they sufficiently profitable? Before you answer that, you need to have a close look at your costs. Here we would recommend the services of a good accountant or book-keeper – someone trained to be completely dispassionate about overheads, materials, time spent and costs incurred on specific jobs. So let's assume that you've done this and that cost-wise you are running a pretty tight ship. Yet certain jobs still look poor earners. What do you do? Obviously you need to increase your prices. This may well be the solution but it may also drive clients away.

A more subtle approach may be to take a closer look at what you provide and its per-

▲ **Commercial photographers don't just sell photography, they also sell ideas and solutions to problems. This is basically a pack shot (that is, we need to see the product itself in detail), but STEVE BICKNELL has used colour gels and the Hosemaster fibre-optic lighting system to create something special for Nintendo. The Hosemaster 'skimmer' tool was used round the edges and the 'probe' tool to splash light onto key areas of the fascia. The result is a good balance between being too obvious and being too clever, which might have meant that special effects or whatever, distracted from the product itself.**

of the industrial and business community to promote itself, its products and its services. Such demand patterns can be a very unpredictable. It will pay to stick close to your clients (and potential clients), try to anticipate their needs and modify the product you offer accordingly.

To pose the second question about the products you offer, we might return to the analogy of buying a car. The customer is faced with a variety of choice. Why should he buy one make rather than another? Or, for that matter, why should he bother with your salesroom at all? Like selling cars, photography is a highly competitive field. What do you offer that sets you apart from your competitors? Do you have an edge? Here the quality of the work you do is paramount. This is where the hours spent perfecting techniques and testing materials can really pay off. Because there's nothing like superb quality to set you apart from competitors and justify higher prices. But, thankfully for those of us who find it difficult to achieve, outstanding creative quality is not the end of the story.

Good service is also vital. In fact, for many clients, provided that work is to a consistent professional standard, service – reliability, a good working relationship, honesty, enthusiasm and a determination to meet the brief – are

'My clients use me not because I'm a better photographer than anyone else, but because they like working with me. People like to feel comfortable.'

Carl Lyttle, advertising photographer

ceived value to the client. In other words, could you add value to your products? Think about the end use of the photographs you take. For example, suppose you are doing product photography for your client's sales reps to show to customers. The end product is a sales leaflet. Could you offer to produce this yourself, perhaps using photoleaflets? Is there a chance that these same images could be displayed at exhibitions or sales reception areas? If you feel your job ends with the creation of the image, you may be missing out on the lion's share of the profit.

As we'll be discussing next, when you really get close to understanding the promotional needs of your clients, all sorts of opportunities will arise. For any image you create, the potential for adding value is boundless. And as long as you come up with the ideas and retain a measure of involvement, then the earning power of your work will increase.

It goes without saying that none of this is possible without building the right relationship with your clients. Who are these important people? How can we increase our influence and, if necessary, how can we find more of them? Whatever level of the business you work at, there's usually someone who has the final decision on whether or not you are hired for a job. Sometimes the relationship is simple: one-to-one with the actual decision maker. More often you will liaise with someone who reports to someone else higher up the ladder; this may lead to the tricky business of working for two bosses. Try to understand the structure of your client company. Involve the senior person whenever you can, but always be loyal to your direct contact and be careful not to alienate them by appearing to go over their heads. That way, he or she will support your case in internal meetings you may be excluded from.

Above all, try to determine the needs of your client and whether your work satisfies these needs. This is not as easy as it sounds. Several factors get in the way of effective communication. At worst, you may have completely the wrong impression of what your client thinks and unless you ask the right questions and listen carefully, you may not read the warning signs that your work is off track.

Then again, your client may not have defined fully what the objectives are. Don't assume that he has a clear vision of what he wants. He may be looking to you for ideas and new directions, and this is where your enthusiasm and creativity can really pay dividends. A thorough discussion of the project will sort out ideas and reduce the likelihood of problems occurring later.

Finally, while we all appreciate praise, it doesn't teach us much. So while it's important to know that your client liked the job, don't be

too easily satisfied. Explain that you are always striving to improve your standards and service to clients, so any constructive comments would be highly valued.

Of course, all this depends on building the right relationship in the first place. Try to remember that however unreasonable they may sometimes seem, clients are also human beings. They have their own problems and their own needs. So be prepared to listen and offer support and reassurance. They may value your work but if they also value your advice and friendship, then your business relationship is much more secure. In business, your client base is your most important asset – so look after it carefully. But unless you've got more work than you can handle, you may also need to extend this base. In the next section we shall consider ways of doing this.

▲ **PETER DAZELEY runs a very successful commercial business, concentrating mainly on advertising work. Yet he still finds time for personal projects like this beautiful instant print emulsion transfer, which is part of a series. Personal work like this plays an important role in Dazeley's portfolio. Examples of commissioned work demonstrate to clients that he can work successfully to a brief, personal work shows that he is a photographer in his own right – able to experiment and develop a personal style.**

Reaching the client

So you have a product for which there is a demand – and you're nothing less than a creative wizzard. Now comes the bit that you may not be so good at: marketing and sales. No matter how good the service is, it has got to be sold to succeed

▲ When visiting clients, MIKE HEMSLEY of Walter Gardiner Photography, takes a portable lightbox. His 5x4 mounted transparencies are not shown in any particular order. Rather, he first talks to the client to discover what is required, then shows only the most appropriate work.

Whether you like it or not, the only way to success in commercial photography is through sales. The trouble is that for many photographers, the creative business of taking pictures and the hard realities of selling, don't seem to mix. The solution may be to hire a salesman or a photographic agent: someone who has no emotional involvement in your photography and whose only aim is to make money for you both. But whether or not you decide to take this route, it will pay you to think carefully about some of the principles of sales and marketing. So read on.

First of all let's try to classify all the existing and potential buyers of your work. In simplified terms, clients run on a continuum from hot to cold. At the hot end are your long-term existing clients – people who like your work, have used it successfully, and with whom you have built up a close working relationship. At the cold end are potential buyers who know nothing about you or your work.

Any sales or marketing exercise can be seen as a process of warming up potential clients, moving them up the continuum from cold to hot. It's important to realise that, because then you'll stop seeing presentations or promotions which don't result in an immediate commission, as a frustrating waste of time. Any exposure of your work to potential clients, makes them that bit more receptive in future. In the persuasion game, familiarity helps to break down the barriers of sales resistance.

Think about that. If you need a plumber, your first choice is likely to be the most familiar, someone who has worked for you before and done a good job. Secondly, you might opt for a plumber recommended by a friend – a sort of second-hand familiarity. Thirdly, you might turn to Yellow Pages and pick someone who lives locally and has a reassuringly businesslike advertisement. Alternatively, if you decide to use a big company, it might be because persistent advertising has made the name more familiar.

Let's start at the cold end of the scale. The obvious advantage is that there are many more potential leads. The trouble is, in fact, that there are too many. To give us a reasonable chance of success we need to narrow the field down in a process sometimes called 'targeting'.

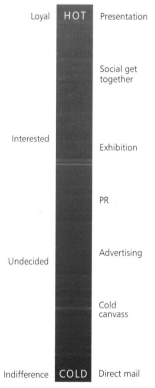

◄ When building work slowed down in the construction industry, NORMAN CHILDS switched to photographing interiors, targeting suppliers of floor coverings, lighting installations, furnishings and so on. Childs has little faith in direct mail, preferring to telephone potential clients direct, explaining who he is, who he has worked for, and asking for an appointment. Sample prints are sent only if an appointment cannot be made.

Long - Term
Existing Clients

Loyal	HOT	Presentation
		Social get together
Interested		Exhibition
		PR
		Advertising
Undecided		Cold canvass
Indifference	COLD	Direct mail

Potential
Clients

▲ 'Any sales or marketing exercise can be seen as a process of warming up potential clients, moving them along the continuum from cold to hot.'

There are many ways of doing this: here are three methods proven to work by photographers.

The first is simply to pick up the telephone and introduce yourself to potential clients. This takes a bit of nerve and can obviously be very frustrating without some very effective targeting. One method is to study business journals and the financial press. Look for companies who are active in the field that interests you, making particular note of new contracts and top staff appointments. Remember that the aim is simply to gain an appointment to show your work to the buyer. Make a one-to-one meeting your prime objective; if that fails, then your fall-back is to send sample prints. If you do send prints, then always follow up with a sec-

ond call, gauging their reaction and hopefully, securing that vital appointment. Handled with sufficient confidence, the direct telephone route is proven to work even with large national companies. Compared to some sales approaches, it's cheap and it's positive – you know at once whether you have struck lucky.

The second method is more appropriate to local clients. Again, it's cheap, very positive, but it involves a fair amount of nerve. What you do is pick an industrial estate and simply go round knocking on doors with your portfolio. The big advantage is that you've missed out the approach stage altogether: you're there, on the spot, and ready to take commissions. Because they need to communicate quickly, photographers who use this method, have

▶ Mail shots work best when repeated. When promoting heavily to maintain orders, Steve Bicknell sent out a special picture each month to existing and potential clients. An accompanying letter explained the picture and kept clients up to date with studio news and services. Bicknell's 'Shot of the Month' became an effective means of keeping the studio's name to the fore.

APPLIED MATERIALS
Implant Division

Shot of the Month

STEVE BICKNELL
INDUSTRIAL & ADVERTISING
PHOTOGRAPHY
——— (0403) 784311 ———

found it best to show printed samples of their work in use: sales leaflets, brochures, magazine covers and so on. Since this type of cold calling is a bit hit and miss, it's usually more effective to show buyers the end product so that they can think, 'Yes, we could do with some leaflets like that, they look good and would help sell our products ...' Once you've captured their interest by showing them something they can relate to, then by all means back it up with samples of your original photography.

The third method is to cold call by telephone from a business directory, Yellow Pages or similar target list. You could do this yourself, but if it's a large list from which you only expect a small percentage of success, then you could hire someone part-time to make the calls for you. Again, the objective is to secure an appointment, with sending prints as a fall-back. You could start your telesales person on an hourly rate, then, if he or she is doing well, offer a bonus for each appointment secured.

WALTER
GARDINER
PHOTOGRAPHY

ADVERTISING
INDUSTRIAL
ARCHITECTURAL

SOUTHDOWNVIEW
ROAD
WORTHING
BN14 8NL
FAX (0903) 820830

TELEPHONE
(0903)
200528

AUGUST
Su M Tu W Th F S
30 31   1
2   3   4   5   6   7   8
9   10 11 12 13 14 15
16 17 18 19 20 21 22
23 24 25 26 27 28 29

◀ MIKE HEMSLEY **also believes in repeat mail shots. At Walter Gardiner Photography, they chose a calendar theme – monthly pictures culminating with a Christmas shot of all the studio photographers dressed up as Victorian carol singers! These were sent to existing clients and a prospect list put together by a specialist direct mail company.**

As we have said before, every sales or marketing exercise is part of the process of moving clients from the cold to the hot end of the continuum. Because what we really want isn't just a one-off commission, it's long-term, loyal clients who will provide the regular work on which we can build a sound business. In this context lots of different activities can help. Remember that the aim is to make potential clients more familiar with your name and your work, because familiarity breaks down sales resistance. Publicity can be valuable: pictures and articles in magazines or your local newspaper (remember to insist on a credit for your pictures — it is now your legal right). Winning competitions, awards or qualifications, can also help establish familiarity, but remember to let people know, both directly and by sending press releases to magazines or your local press.

This is not the time for false modesty.

One proven way of letting people know about yourself, your achievements and your work, is direct mail. But first a word about mailing lists. Whether it's rented, borrowed from a directory, or just scribbled on a piece of paper, everything starts with a list. The trick is to get the right list: one that is current and relevant to your needs. It also needs to be manageable in size. Because direct mail is really just an approach, designed to warm up the client and make your work more familiar, the actual business comes from a follow-up telephone call. So keep your list small enough to service it effectively.

Another tip is to repeat the prescription. You'll very rarely see (or remember for that matter) an advertisement that appears only

▶ While working on another job, the author received this sample card through the post in the same envelope as a PR picture. What better example of getting your name around? Manchester-based BILL PRUDOM is a GP commercial photographer doing mostly PR work. He stresses that the business is sold on service, 'nobody wants to wait more than 24 hours for a job,' he suggests. Using local pro lab PCL, he usually turns work around in four hours. The laminated card cost him £800 for 1000 copies, including the services of a professional designer to put it together. 'We like to let the card do the talking for us,' says Prudom.

once. It's the same with direct mail: a planned campaign, say over six months, is usually more effective than a single mail shot. It takes time and persistence for something or someone to become familiar. To convince a new client to have enough faith to take the big step of hiring you, may take a considerable time and all the marketing and sales techniques we have described.

An alternative approach is to hire a direct marketing company to do the job for you. They will source the list, help you with the content of your mail shot, and follow up on the telephone. But try to avoid paying straight fees. Any company that believes in its abilities, will tie pay-

ment to a certain guaranteed level of results, ie appointments made. That way you should be able to work out in advance what each appontment is going to cost you.

Are there any short cuts? Certainly. Remember what we said about choosing a plumber? Short of calling someone who has worked for you before, the next best thing is to contact a plumber who has been recommended to you. Recommendation can be a powerful force in commercial photography too. But isn't recommendation something that just happens, something out of our control? Not entirely. By carefully nurturing our con-

SANDERS NICOLSON 071-739 6987

▲ For several years Frome-based photographer PETER LOWRY sent his clients Christmas cards featuring caricatures of himself by cartoonist Richard Pearce. The response, he says, was fantastic. The cards cost around £400 – including the artist's fee – for 250 copies.

▲ Advertising photographer PETER DAZELEY also sends Christmas cards to his clients. Inside is a complete list of credits: photographer, designer, model, stylist etc. No such thing as a free Christmas card!

tacts (ie continually reminding them of our presence and availability), we can encourage recommendation and referrals. As they say, 'It's not what you know, it's who you know.' In fact this process — sometimes known as 'networking' — is one of the most effective ways of winning new business.

A network is a carefully developed group of contacts who may be useful to your business. It will certainly include existing clients, but will also extend to valuable contacts outside your active client base. For example, contacts in the press and business magazines could be useful: not only can they give exposure to your work, they may also recommend you to buyers. Colleagues in professional associations can also be helpful. Or you may link up with more formalised networks, such as your local chamber of commerce, golf club or charitable association. A network usually has a social aspect, the great advantage being that this gives you the opportunity to increase that all important familiarity in an informal setting. It's surprising how many valuable initial contact are made at social gatherings.

In fact some photographers increase their chances of strengthening contacts by holding open days, wine and cheese evenings and exhibitions. By inviting potential as well as existing clients and other valuable contacts, they encourage introductions and referrals.

But how ever valuable such activities may be in 'warming up' potential clients and increasing familiarity, most actual commissions depend on a good presentation. In fact, as we have indicated, besides making clients feel good about using you, the ultimate purpose of most promotional activity is to secure face-to-face appointments.

How should you approach that all important interview? The vital thing to remember is that your presentation should be much more than a performance to show how clever and talented you are. It should show how your photography can meet the needs and solve the communication problems of your prospective client. That's why, when approaching local businesses, we advised showing sales leaflets or other printed examples of your work in use — material the client could relate to.

It's the difference between what marketing people call 'demand-pull' and 'supply-push'. Tapping demand is always more effective than pushing supply. So do your homework: make sure you find out as much as you can about the prospect, his business, other photographers he may have used, and likely requirements, before the interview. Then tailor the work you present to what is likely to be the most relevant. You may even prefer not to open your portfolio until 10 or 15 minutes into the interview, using this time to discuss the requirements of your client. That way, you can play your portfolio like a hand of cards, showing first the type of images most likely to fit the bill.

Good editing is vital. Don't necessarily back your own judgment. Try out your pictures on friends and colleagues to see which images have the most impact. Most photographers agree that you should start with something stunning, but opinions differ as to the number of pictures you should show. The general consensus is that 30 is the absolute limit — normally you should be able to make your point with ten. Depending on the sophistication of the buyer, laminated prints or mounted transparencies (no smaller than 5x4) should be equally effective in proving the technical quality of your photography.

Finally, a word about enthusiasm. Some photographers are diffident about their work — almost as if they are embarrassed to show it. Don't be. The client regards you as an expert (why else would he be talking to you?), so don't create doubt by being anything less than confident in your own abilities. On the other hand, enthusiasm is contagious, and may well carry the day with an uncertain prospect. And when the right moment comes, don't be afraid to ask for work. Nobody enjoys rejection, but if you can't handle it, you shouldn't be in business. The motto of the successful sales person is, 'Never be afraid to expose yourself to the possibility of making a sale.'

So you have identified a market and done your bit to persuade the client that you are the one for the job. But how much do you charge? And are you sure that the bill will produce a profit after all your costs are accounted for?

Staying alive

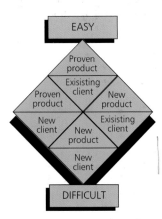

▲ Use this classic product marketing diagram to remind yourself of the easiest ways to win new business. Tried and tested products are easiest to sell to existing clients, who know and like your work. The hardest thing is to try something new on new clients.

OK, let's say your presentation went well and your new client is ready to give you a commission. Sooner or later the inevitable question comes up, 'What's it going to cost me?' We have suggested that commercial photography ought to be sales-lead. But of course, sales alone are not enough to ensure that your business stays alive. For that we need profits. So the real value of a job is the difference between what you charge and the costs that job has to carry.

That might seem pretty obvious, but the trap many photographers fall into is underestimating costs. That's why it's usually sensible to have someone else – a business partner, book keeper or accountant – to look after the cost side of the business.

Getting the price right is one of the key factors to success in business. The worst thing is to start too low – if you've got your sums wrong, it can be very difficult then to convince clients that they ought to pay more. On the other hand, if your prices are on the high side and you are encountering resistance, it's not unreasonable to discount slightly, as long as you let your clients know you are doing them a favour. So where do you start? Basically there are two ways of looking at pricing. The first is from the buyer's viewpoint: how much is he or she prepared to pay? Not an easy question to answer, but you can sometimes go some of the way with questions like, 'What sort of budget do you have for this job?' Clients will not always be prepared to answer, but if you don't ask, you don't get. And you'll never know how much you could have made.

Behind this approach to pricing is your market value. How does your work compare to other photographers your client may have dealt with? Whatever level of the business you work at – local, national or a mixture of the two – it will pay you to find out what your direct competitors are charging. Remember, your client is not particularly interested in what it costs you to do a job, more whether he's paying the 'going rate' for photography of a certain quality.

So we could say, 'Charge as much as the market will stand.' Make this your optimum price, then work out a minimum based on costs.

The first step is material costs: film, paper,

processing, presentation materials and so on. These are sometimes called 'cost of working' and should be fairly straightforward to work out. You should also add in other personal expenses, such as travel, any accommodation necessary and so on. Any equipment or studio hire should be added in at this point.

Next you need to build in overheads. These are continuous expenses that you incur whether you are working or not: studio rents and rates, power bills, staff costs, insurance, stationery, promotional costs, depreciation of capital equipment (cameras, studio flash, processing equipment, computers, fax machine and so on), accountancy fees, legal fees … As we've mentioned before, it's a good idea to sort this out with an accountant – most accountants take pride in being able to save you at least enough to be able to pay their fees! From these costs you should be able to calculate a monthly, weekly and even daily figure. In theory, every job you do should earn enough to carry a fair proportion of your overheads.

Finally, what about you? Don't you want to earn a living? Work out how much you need to lead a decent life and break this down to a daily rate. Apply this to the time you estimate the job will take, then add in direct costs and a share of overheads – the result should be the minimum you are prepared to accept.

All this sounds good on paper and it really is important to be aware of the costs a job has to carry – nearly always more than you imagined. But in the real world it is the first pricing method – your perceived market value – that will determine how much you charge.

To simplify matters, many commercial photographers – particularly in the advertising field – have a general price tag known as their 'day rate'. This is what it costs to hire that photographer for a day, with direct costs and expenses usually charged on top. The day rate tends to reflect the best price the photographer thinks he or she can charge, though when work is scarce, it may well be discounted.

Let's assume you are doing it all right: building a strong customer base, winning new business and charging good prices. What can possibly go wrong? The answer is, not very much. And this is why, in good times, many photographers get away with not being very astute business people.

It's when things get tougher – fewer jobs around, reduced budgets, clients who want special deals – that many photographers come unstuck. As with any business, the key to survival is accurate information. When business gets marginal, it becomes vital to know where costs can be cut, which jobs are the most profitable and so on. Once you get into the habit of

tight business control, you will find that the picture becomes clearer and it's easier to make the right decisions. As we've already mentioned, it's also vital to stay close to your clients and try to understand what's happening to their businesses. This should enable you to anticipate opportunities and make provision for disappointments.

Finally, with a clear picture of what your business is doing and an understanding of what future demand may be, you'll be better placed to think about investment and expansion. But tread carefully: the decision to expand has made some photographers rich but it has caused others to founder. Remember, increasing your overheads by employing staff, borrowing money, leasing capital equipment or moving to larger premises, means extra responsibility and a constant demand on turnover.

Can you generate enough sales, and if you can, isn't it possible you might do better by staying small and covering the most profitable jobs yourself? Only you can decide.

▲ Sometimes a photographer needs to move with the market. Newcastle-based DANNY MADDOCKS cut his teeth on heavy industrial work: coal, steel, ship building and so on. With the decline of these industries and the growing accent on the hi-tech areas of business, nowadays Maddocks is more often photographing computer terminals than industrial processes. This shot for Kelly Packaging is a typical example.

Basics

This chapter is not just about the nuts and bolts of photography. Of course it's important to understand the basics – without them you'd be lost. But even more important is to know when to use which technique and how to put techniques together in a seamless manner that doesn't distract from the intention of the picture. Or, for that matter, when to opt for a classically simple solution which allows the form of the subject itself to shine through – as with Tessa Traeger's beautiful study of a Chanterelle fungus shown opposite...

Professional photographers occasionally express concern that the automation of modern camera equipment is allowing amateurs to work to professional standards. They feel threatened. But true pros can set themselves apart in a number of ways – a prime example being in the quality of the work they produce

A question of quality

There is a popular myth that photography has now become so automated, almost anyone can pick up a modern camera and take decent pictures. On a modern 35mm SLR (or even an automatic viewfinder-type compact) everything is taken care of: exposure is read and controlled by a complex array of sensors, while autofocus has now become so efficient that moving subjects can be tracked and held in focus. Even the tricky area of flash photography have been automated with 'dedicated' flashguns and — on some cameras — a built-in flash pops up and fires only when needed. Nowadays you don't even have to remember to set the film speed or wind on. In fact, with everything made so easy, it's surprising that so many people still manage to make a living from photography! The answer, of course, is that access to the right tools doesn't necessarily mean that anyone can do a good job. It's the same in other fields: buying modern hi-fi and recording equipment doesn't automatically qualify us to become sound recording engineers.

Taking a really good photograph – particularly in the commercial field – can be hugely difficult. There are so many things that can go wrong. Those doyens of photography, David Bailey and Terrence Donovan, once sat down and tried to work out all the things that could go wrong on a shoot: camera jams; model doesn't turn up; art director has a tantrum; assistant knocks over the light; weather turns nasty … When they reached 1000 they gave up!

If you watch a top food photographer at work in the studio, you begin to appreciate why everything seems to move so slowly, why an apparently simple shot may take three days. Achieving really stunning results depends on so many factors: the right equipment and materials; precise composition and styling; meticulous lighting; constant attention to 1001 details. This may also explain why, although all photographers need these qualities to be successful, food specialists seem to have more than their fair share of diligence, self-possession and obsessive attention to the job in hand – what business commentators call 'focus'. What such specialists are paid – sometimes very highly – to achieve, is quality. What do we mean by quality? Perhaps the easiest way to define it is to say that if your work lacks quality, that's the

◄ It was well into the night when STEVE BICKNELL took this shot for BOC Special Gases, and he had a plane to catch early next morning. Yet he still managed to pull out the stops and create a high quality picture. Notice how he gives the composition a feeling of depth by keeping light off the foreground. *(See diagram below)*

first thing an experienced buyer will notice. Less experienced buyers will notice too, though they may find it harder to put a finger on what is missing.

Essentially, quality in this context, breaks down into two areas: creative and technical. Often it's difficult to separate the two, and a first-rate photograph will probably score highly in both categories. Creative quality implies that the picture has impact: it stimulates or intrigues the viewer and usually communicates an idea, preferably in an original manner. Technical quality means that the intention of the picture is rendered to the highest possible technical standard. In this book we can show you examples of creative quality and explain some of the thinking that went into creating the picture. But although we can point you in the right direction, we can't really tell you how to achieve it. That's something you can only find out for yourself through experimenting and striving constantly to find better solutions.

With technical quality, it's a different matter. You can make a respectable living in commercial photography without being particularly creative. But if your technical quality lets you down – pictures not quite sharp, lighting flat, exposures slightly off, processing inadequate and so on – then you'll find it difficult to survive. Perhaps surprisingly, first-rate technical quality is what is lacking from the work of most photographic students. Many have interesting, occasionally original, ideas – but the communication process is let down by the way those ideas are executed. Those who

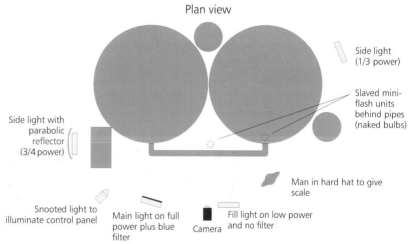

Plan view

Side light with parabolic reflector (3/4 power)

Side light (1/3 power)

Slaved mini-flash units behind pipes (naked bulbs)

Man in hard hat to give scale

Snooted light to illuminate control panel

Main light on full power plus blue filter

Camera

Fill light on low power and no filter

go on to become assistants or photographers in their own right, quickly learn what professional quality is all about.

How can good technical quality be achieved? In photography there are certain fixed laws governing, for example, how light behaves, what lenses can achieve, how colour is reproduced and processing controlled. It's important to understand these rules, but technical quality also depends on experience – taking lots of pictures and analysing the results. That's because photography is a pragmatic process: what's good is what works.

'Once you've used 5x4, you'll never go back...'

Ian McKinnell, architectural photographer

Tools for the job

Knowing how to get the best out the equipment you own is more important than the precise nature of the kit itself. That's not to say that there is usually a right tool for the job

▲ **Hasselblad 205TCC 6x6cm medium format camera: equally at home in the studio or on location, the elegantly designed 'Blad has become the 'workhorse' of many professionals.**

Many years ago, one of the Sunday colour supplements carried out an interesting experiment. It chose six top professional photographers and presented each with the cheapest, most basic, compact camera on the market — one with a less than impressive plastic lens — and instructed them to go out and take publishable pictures. Most of the results were first-class, with one or two of the pros shooting very memorable images. Why did they succeed? Because they understood the limitations of the camera. For example, they knew that the lens would only be capable of taking soft, ill-defined images. So they deliberately chose to take soft, 'impressionistic' pictures – where colour, composition and mood were far more important than sharpness and consistent exposure across the frame.

The moral is that it's not the equipment that counts, it's what you do with it. Of course, the

▲ **A major advantage of camera movements on large format cameras is the ability to reposition the plane of focus in such a way as to give the impression of extended depth of field. But movements can equally be used to suggest a very *narrow* plane of focus. This is the technique PETER DAZELEY has used in this shot for Sales Machine art director Micky Titterton. Dazeley was commissioned to shoot a series of useful objects, including this pencil sharpener, which appeared in a calendar for software company Microsoft. Each is shot with a narrow plane of focus to give continuity of style to the project.**

professionals in our example enjoyed a very loose brief – it would probably have been a different story had they been asked to take quality product shots for a sales brochure or catalogue. So while we shouldn't assume that photography improves in proportion to the amount we spend on cameras, we do need equipment that is capable of achieving the results required for the job. Let's look at the options available.

35mm: the enemy? To some professionals, modern automated 35mm cameras are the enemy. These are the cameras that clients can use and it has to be said that they do. How often do we see clients' photographs – particularly pictures of staff – appearing in brochures, internal publications and even company reports? They may be poorly composed and look a bit stilted, but they are generally sharp and adequately exposed. What's more, they obviously fulfil the most important criterion – acceptability to the client. Photographers themselves are partly to blame. It's often said that 'we need to educate clients', and nowhere is this more important than in areas where they may believe that an outside photographer is unnecessary. Never undervalue, for example, the importance of the humble staff picture or PR shot. As we explain in Chapter 7 People Pictures, by working hard to organise the shot and paying attention to expression and composition, we can make sure the client understands the value of hiring a professional. Having said that, it's perfectly possible to take many types of commercial photography on 35mm. Indeed, most commercial photographers own a 35mm outfit, but apart from jobs such as audiovisual presentations where 35mm slides are needed, they will rarely use it.

There are two reasons for this. The first is technical: larger formats, by recording the image on a larger piece of film, can achieve much higher technical quality (finer grain, better resolution, smoother tonal gradation and so on) – far more image information per shot. Large formats also offer greater flexibility to manage the image through camera movements. Some of these movements are available on a few 35mm lenses, though at a price well beyond the reach of most amateur enthusiast clients.

The second reason is psychological. Since most clients probably own amateur cameras themselves; it does no harm to cultivate a little professional mystique by arriving with lights and big cameras, which look professional, highly technical and, above all, difficult to operate. Finally, if your end-product is in transparency form, even though 35mm slides may be perfectly adequate for reproduction, larger formats are easier to view on a lightbox and look far more impressive to clients.

Medium format: all purpose So-called 'medium format' cameras are designed to accept what is commonly known as 'rollfilm' or 120 film (so named because the usable image area measures 120mm across the film). There is also 220 film which is the same width, but comes in a roll which is double the length of 120, kept to a spool of the same size by doing away with the backing paper which is a feature of 120 film. Originally an amateur format, 120 is now used almost exclusively for professional cameras and a wide range of film types is available, designed with professionals in mind (see Chapter 11 Materials). In addition, most are medium format cameras are equipped with removable film backs, which also enables instant film to be used for checking lighting, exposure and composition.

Within the 120 format, different camera models divide the film in different ways. The classic format of 6x6cm is probably still the most popular, but other formats have arisen mainly because most prints and reproduced pictures, appear in rectangular rather than

▲ Although he began his career as a still life photographer shooting on 5x4, advertising/fashion specialist SANDERS NICOLSON now shoots almost exclusively on 35mm. Modern emulsions give him the quality he needs and a motor-drive is indispensable for the action 'lifestyle' photography he often shoots. This shot for the cover of a German catalogue was 'cross-processed' – transparency film developed in print film chemistry, a technique he often uses for extra pictorial impact.

▲ The Canon EOS-1 35mm SLR is a popular choice for professionals because of its fast and accurate autofocus system and the extensive choice of lenses.

▲ **Horseman LX-C large format 5x4 monorail camera, has precise calibrations for accurate camera movements.**

square shapes. There are other advantages too: for example, 6x4.5cm allows maximum use of most print paper formats and also saves money by giving 15 instead of 12 shots per roll. On the other hand, 6x7cm produces bigger negatives or slides (ie more information per shot) while still conforming more closely to print paper formats. Wider formats such as 6x8cm, 6x9cm (which has the same aspect ratio as 35mm) and even panoramic formats up to 6x17, are also available.

The main advantages of medium over large format cameras are portability, convenience, cost savings in materials, and to a lesser extent, the wider range of lenses available (such as extreme wide angle). As a result, many commercial studios use medium format as the main 'workhorse', especially for location work. Medium format cameras can also be used for many studio jobs – some are even equipped with camera movements, though these not as comprehensive as those available with large format technical cameras.

Often the choice between medium and large format can be a matter of personal preference. As we said earlier, it's not the equipment that counts, it's what you do with it. For example, some photographers have successfully used medium format for the type of industrial work where, formerly, nothing less than large format would have been considered. In fact, if you had to choose only one type of camera for general commercial work, we would advise medium format. As with any equipment purchase, choosing the right camera has to be a compromise between what you feel you need and what you can sensibly afford. But don't be too impressed by special features or electronic wizardry. Bear in mind that the most important factors are less easy for the salesman to demonstrate: lens quality, reliability and durability.

Large format: the ultimate Large format or 'view' cameras take some getting use to and certainly look complicated. For this reason, many photographers find elaborate excuses to avoid having to use them. On the other hand, some practitioners are so convinced of their advantages that they use nothing else. We don't propose to give detailed instructions on how to use large format – better to go on a course or teach yourself from a handbook. Rather we'd prefer to explain some of the principles and, hopefully, alleviate the fears some photographers have at the very idea of con-

'Overhead, bright sunshine makes me panic. I prefer overcast skies and I like to shoot early or late in the day. Fortunately, with the weather we get in this country, dark cloudy skies have become my trademark...'

Sanders Nicolson

fronting these big cameras.

The construction of a view camera is quite simple. In fact, the basic design hasn't changed since the early days of photography back in the last century. There are four principle elements:
• A lens panel which contains the lens, aperture control and shutter
• A viewing/film panel on which is spring-mounted a ground glass viewing screen, which can be pushed back to allow a film plate to be inserted on exactly the same plane.
• A light-tight bellows to connect the two panels.
• A rail system (called a 'monorail' if it is a single rail) on which the two panels are mounted allowing them to be moved forward and back independently, while remaining connected by the bellows.

In addition, both the lens and the viewing/film panel are mounted on 'standards' – usually L-shaped or U-shaped – which allow each panel independently to be raised or lowered, tilted up or down, or swung from left to right. If the film and lens panels are kept in exact alignment, then a view camera functions just like any other camera. The only difference is that the lens is focused by turning a knob which brings the panels closer together or further apart.

It is with movement of the lens and film standards that things start to get interesting. Movements have two basic aims: to control the plane of focus and to alter the appearance of perspective. Let's look at what can be done:
• **Tilt** This is particularly useful in achieving overall sharpness for tabletop product shots. With any lens depth of field can be increased by selecting a smaller aperture, but with a view camera, an additional method is available which places the plane of focus in such a way as to increase the apparent depth of field. Normally the plane of focus is parallel to the camera back; but suppose the camera is aimed downwards at 45°, by tilting the lens in relation to the back so that it is parallel with your subject, you can relocate the plane of focus so that the image is rendered sharp without the need for a very small aperture. In addition, tilting can eliminate or exaggerate the distortion of perspective which occurs when you move close to a subject.
• **Swing** If your subject or group of subjects, moves diagonally away from the lens, then swivelling the lens panel in the same direction can ensure overall sharpness from front to back by, again, altering the plane of focus. Swing can also be used to control perspective distor-

◄ For reasons of cost and convenience, editorial/architectural photographer JULIAN NIEMAN uses medium format 6x7 (with movements) for most of the pictures he takes for clients such as *Country Life* magazine. However, for this beautiful interior of Syon House, West London, he chose a 5x4 camera for the extra control it gives, ensuring that the verticals stay vertical and that the ornate ceiling could be included through use of vertical shift. No extra lighting was needed – in fact you could say that the shot was lit by Robert Adam, who designed the room. Staff on *Country Life* were impressed too, and used it for their front cover.

tion or to achieve a distorted 'wide angle' effect.

• **Rise and fall** Whether your subject is a bottle or a tall building, if you need the vertical lines of the subject to remain vertical, then this is achieved by raising or lowering the lens panel, making sure that both lens and film panel remain parallel with the subject.

In effect, camera movements offer the photographer incredible versatility in the quest for technical perfection. Modern view cameras offer other benefits too. Most are modular in construction and this allows extra bellows to be added (for close-up work), lenses to be changed and different film backs to be added (for 4x5in or 10x8in film sheets, instant film, or even the more economical 120 rollfilm).

Disadvantages of view cameras stem mainly from their bulk and complexity. You'll certainly need a sturdy tripod or studio camera support system: hand-holdable they're not. You may also feel that the lack of mobility limits their use for shots involving people. But for studio product shots, large-scale industrial or accurate architectural work, they have no equal.

If you're still not sure, hire a decent monorail outfit for a week or two and play with it.

Seeing the light

Where would we all be without light? An understanding of its nature – and how to control it – is one thing photographers should not be in the dark on

Without light there can be no photography. Everything depends on it. The nature of a photograph is completely governed by the quality and intensity of light and the way it behaves. And that includes not just whether your exposure is correct, but also how sharp the image appears, whether colours are strong or muted, and the mood or atmosphere of the picture. So it will pay you to look around and take careful note of the way light behaves and different surfaces reflect it, whether in the studio or at locations both inside and out. You won't need a camera for this, just a highly critical eye. As Cartier-Bresson is reputed to have said, 'Some of my best pictures were taken without a camera'. But remember, you need to concentrate, because in normal circumstances, the eye/brain combination relaxes, averaging out the information it receives in a process known as 'accommodation'.

Any type of naturally occurring light – direct or diffused sunlight, moonlight, windowlight, firelight and so on – can be recreated in the studio, or enhanced on location. By the same token, any naturally occurring distractions, such as uneven illumination, unwanted shadows or colour casts, can be controlled or eliminated. But it all starts with seeing: unless you look carefully and become aware of the way light behaves, you will never learn to control it. What you will notice, at different times of the day, for example, is that the way light illuminates objects and creates shadows can differ enormously. We can break down these differences – which are the same for any light source – into three categories: intensity, quality and colour.

Light intensity Intensity of light is the most obvious. On a bright, clear day at noon we can

Fall-off in light intensity, as set out by the Inverse Square Law

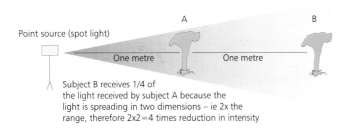

Point source (spot light)

A

B

One metre

One metre

Subject B receives 1/4 of the light received by subject A because the light is spreading in two dimensions – ie 2x the range, therefore 2x2 = 4 times reduction in intensity

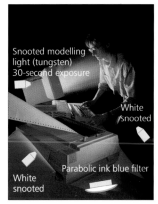

Snooted modelling
light (tungsten)
30-second exposure

White
snooted

Parabolic ink blue filter

White
snooted

◄ STEVE BICKNELL took this
shot during a workshop at an
Infot conference for industrial
photographers. He wanted to
show how the standard picture
of a computer operator can be
made more dramatic. Notice
how the paper spewing out of
the printer in the foreground
helps to give the picture depth
and leads the eye in to the
main subject: the operator. A
broad, parabolic flash with
blue filter was used to light
the equipment, while two
highly directional, snooted
white flash heads light the
operator and keyboard. The
glare coming apparently from
the screen is produced by a
tungsten 'effect light' which
required a separate exposure
of 30 seconds, during which
time, light was kept off the
operator with a black mask.
(See lighting sketch below)

▲ A flash meter like this
Minolta Autometer IV, is
essential for accurate exposure
calculations.

see everything very accurately and in full
colour. However, towards evening, things
become less distinct and colours begin to look
dark and muddy. Artificial light sources
behave in the same way, with one important
additional qualification: this is that light from
sources closer to us than the sun (eg electric
light bulbs, flash heads, candles), falls off in
intensity the further the subject is moved away.

The degree to which this fall-off occurs is
defined by the 'Inverse Square Law' which
states that when a subject is illuminated by a
point source of light, the intensity of light at its
surface is inversely proportional to the square
of its distance from the light source. In practice
this means that by, say, moving a lamp to twice
its original distance from the subject, illumination is reduced to a quarter. Conversely, moving the lamp to half its original distance from
the subject, gives four times as much illumination. Light fall-off is much less noticeable to the
human eye than it is to the camera: this is why
to make a photograph appear 'normal' rather
than shadowy, it is usually necessary to light
the background as well as the subject.

The important advantage of artificial light
sources, such as studio flash or tungsten lamps,
is that their intensity is a fairly constant, fixed
quantity, whereas sunlight, of course, is infinitely variable. In the studio, this means that
the photographer can build up lighting, rather
as an artist might with paints, safe in the
knowledge each light will remain constant.
Outdoors, artificial lighting can also be used,
but the sudden appearance or disappearance
of the sun still creates problems.

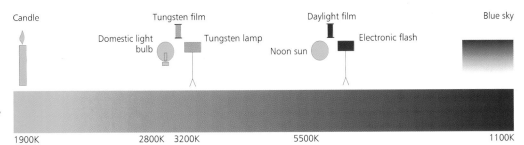

Colour Temperature

| Candle | Domestic light bulb | Tungsten film | Tungsten lamp | Noon sun | Daylight film | Electronic flash | Blue sky |

1900K   2800K 3200K   5500K   1100K

Light intensity is measured with a light meter (called a flash meter when designed for use with electronic flash). Accurate measurement is important because films are designed to perform best within a relatively narrow ranges of light intensity between the lightest and darkest parts of a picture. For example, a typical outdoor scene might have a brightness range of 12:1, whereas colour negative film accurately records only a range of around 3:1 (beyond that highlights 'burn out' and shadows 'fill-in' and lack tonal gradation).

In the studio, this range of light intensity – sometimes called the lighting ratio – is much easier to control than it is outdoors. The output of most electronic flash heads is adjustable in steps, and – remembering the Inverse Square Law – lamps can be moved closer or further away from the subject. Finally, light can be 'filled in' (ie the lighting ratio reduced) by using reflectors – a technique which can also be used outdoors to reduce the high lighting ratio of sunlight.

Quality of light The 'quality' of light refers to the directness of its wavelengths. The 'point sources' we mentioned above, are harsh direct lights such as direct sunlight, a naked, clear glass electric bulb, or a spotlight. Direct light produces hard, dark shadows and bright highlights, which can wash out colour completely from parts of the subject. For this reason, direct light (focused spotlights for example) is normally used not as a main light, but to highlight certain features of the subject, or to light the background. However, in varying degrees, direct light can also be diffused by any translucent substance, so that it becomes scattered and illuminates the subject more evenly. This happens naturally on a cloudy day or when the sun shines at an angle (early morning or late afternoon) and is diffused through a greater part of the earth's atmosphere.

In the studio, or at home, light can be diffused either by reflecting (or 'bouncing') it off a light-coloured, reflective surface (eg wall, ceiling, reflector or purpose-made 'umbrella'), or by covering it with a translucent substance such as tracing paper, frosted glass or a translucent plastic such as frosted acetate or mylar. Diffused light is preferred for most commercial jobs because it produces softer shadows and more even colour saturation. With studio-based photographers, this accounts for the popularity of large banks of electronic flash heads housed in a box covered with a translucent diffusing material – often known as 'soft boxes'. These units – available in many shapes and sizes – give a soft, even, diffused light, with the added advantage that their square shape produces clean reflections such as you might get from a window. For simple product shots, they are also quick and simple to use as a main light, producing good professional quality with only a single reflector to 'fill in' the shadow areas.

Colour of light 'Colour temperature' refers to the actual colour bias of apparently white light. We say 'apparently' because, due to the 'accommodation' we mentioned earlier, human vision does not distinguish readily between variations in colour temperature. For example, most people (photographers excepted!) don't notice much difference between daylight outdoors and an artificially-lit sitting room. Naturally they can see that daylight

'A studio photographer's job is to simulate natural light in a false situation.'

Carl Lyttle, advertising photographer

tends to be much brighter, but they are generally unaware that electric light bulbs give a warm, slightly orange-coloured light and that this makes a considerable difference to the way they perceive colours.

Film, of course, is not influenced by accommodation, and therefore registers a dramatic difference in these two lighting conditions. Since flash light is close in colour temperature to daylight, and tungsten studio lights to the orange-tinted domestic lighting, most films are balanced to register whites as white either in daylight or in tungsten conditions, and are designated accordingly (see Chapter 11 Materials). When used with electronic flash, daylight film will register very slightly too blue (due in part to the ultraviolet light created by the flash), so this is usually corrected by a special filter either

◄ Sometimes it pays to think laterally when faced with a lighting problem. When Southern Water commissioned MIKE HEMSLEY to take pictures of Redhill Service Reservoir, he was lead to believe that all the shots would be exterior. Consequently he left his lights behind. However, this underground chamber caught his eye so he improvised with three naked light bulbs powered by a small generator, which the site contractors were using. By hiding bulbs behind three of the pillars, Helmsley created dominant forward shadows, and probably produced a more interesting shot than he might have achieved with conventional lighting. Exposure times were 30, 40 and 60 seconds.

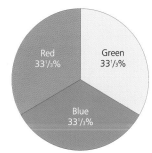

Daylight at 5500K

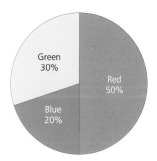

Tungsten light at 3200K

▲ Daylight on an average day, at 5500 Kelvin, comes the closest to what we perceive as 'white light'. On the other hand, a tungsten studio lamp at around 3200 Kelvin shows a much higher proportion of red light and less blue.

on the camera or over the flash head. Alternatively, the image can be 'warmed up' using yellow or gold coloured reflectors.

The term 'colour temperature' is generally used in the search for the type of white light which, when matched with the correct film and exposure, produces the most 'natural' colours (an approximation of how most people would agree that certain colours, such as green grass or flesh tones, should appear in photographs). However, we should also consider how more strongly coloured light can affect results. Artificially, light can be coloured by colour filters— either over the light source or in front of the camera lens — but colours in a picture can also be affected by naturally occurring coloured reflections. Again, the effects of accommodation can make these colour casts difficult to spot, but care needs to be taken

when photographing differently coloured objects close together or against coloured backgrounds. Flesh tones and food are particularly susceptible, mainly because with these subjects, most viewers have a low tolerance of any colour deviation from what they regard as 'normal'.

As we have said, commercial photography is all about control. So, depending on the effect required, coloured filters over lamps (known as 'gels') and coloured reflectors, can be used either to bring a picture as close as possible to 'natural' colouring, or to add colour to an otherwise drab subject.

The danger here is in overdoing it. Ideally, just enough extra colour should be added to give the shot excitement, while retaining sufficient natural colour to ensure that the subject remains recognisable.

the Studio

Lease, rent, buy? Commercial photographers regularly need a workplace in which they can set up the shot, but the precise nature of your clients and their products will decide which option fits your business best

Since the earliest days of photography, to professional photographers having a studio has been almost as important as having a camera. The majority of Victorian professionals were portrait photographers, so the word 'studio' obviously derives from its use as a painter's workplace – at that time both photographers and painters were competing to capture a good likeness of their sitters. Thus, since painters were there first, the idea of a 'studio' traded on the long tradition of painting, giving the new technology of photography an air of artistic respectability.

There were technical advantages too. A purpose-built studio enabled photographers to ensure that lighting conditions were kept consistently at optimum levels – at first with large windows often north facing, later with artificial lighting. There was also the advantage of having props and backgrounds to hand, not to mention the size of cameras and the hefty clamping apparatus necessary to keep the sitter still for long exposures.

In basic terms, very little has changed. The idea of a studio still carries something of a mystique with clients. And in the technical area, the advantage of being able to control lighting, backgrounds and props, still holds good. Even on the processing side, many commercial studios still keep to the traditional method of running a darkroom next to the studio. The modern commercial studio preserves a link with the past which is also very relevant today – particularly for the type of work that requires elaborate sets, lighting and other non-transportable equipment. Most commercial photographers have a studio, though of course, for those specialising in location work (architectural, industrial, PR and so on), it's quite possible to do without. For those in city areas, it's also possible to hire excellently equipped studios of practically any size, as and when you need one.

But for most, even aside from its usefulness, the studio remains a kind of emotional base. And there's a commercial dimension too: even though you may work on location, most clients expect you to have a studio – it implies a certain seriousness and sense of purpose. So a studio has a certain value as a business asset. But the question is, what is that value and how much of your hard-earned income should you

◀ A slightly glamourised view of the studio area at WALTER GARDINER PHOTOGRAPHY in Worthing – it doesn't normally look as tidy as this! Overleaf we show all the support systems – reception areas, processing and printing, finishing and so on – which enable a busy commercial studio like WGP to function smoothly.

spend on supporting your studio?

When you buy a camera, film, processing or a basic lighting kit, these are necessities rather than business decisions – you could not operate efficiently as a photographer without them. However, buying or renting a studio involves such a variation of possible costs – depending on type, size, fittings and location – that it becomes, at least partly, a business decision. Of course there are basic requirements – you need sufficient space and the facilities to do the type of work for which you have identified a demand. But for most photographic businesses, the studio is a major overhead. And if things go wrong – client companies folding, budgets cut, bad debts and so on – paying studio rent and rates becomes a major headache and probably the principal cause of failure of photographic businesses. So, if you are thinking of taking on your first studio, or perhaps upgrading to a bigger one, it will pay you to proceed with caution.

Try to be realistic. Assess the type of work you are mostly likely to get and plan accordingly. For example, if most of your assignments will be small scale products, pack shots and location work, do you really need a space big enough to photograph cars? As long as your studio can cater for the majority of likely jobs, then for the odd roomset or vehicle, the right space can usually be hired – either a studio or, perhaps, a local hall. In business terms, the work you do pays for the studio; and if you don't get enough big product jobs to cover the extra cost of a bigger studio, then some of that money goes straight down the drain.

Having said that, fortune favours the brave. If you are determined to carry large overheads

◀ GP photographer PETER LOWRY has a very small studio in Frome, Somerset – just the right size for portraiture and photographing small objects. So when he has roomset photography to shoot – like this picture for a bathroom catalogue – he hires the local church hall for a week and constructs the whole set there. It certainly works out cheaper and more convenient than hiring a large purpose-built studio or being committed to a lease.

on your studio, then spend your money on the right address. That means being close to your clients – you might not mind travelling long distances to visit them, but in certain fields, particularly advertising and fashion, your clients may feel differently if it is them doing the travelling. If you are looking for commercial work locally, then it makes sense to locate in a business park or industrial estate.

Your studio is more than just the place where you create images – it's part of the image you project to your clients. It may be an essential part of your business, but don't take it for granted – remember that it can also be a major drain on your resources.

The studio of Walter Gardiner Photography

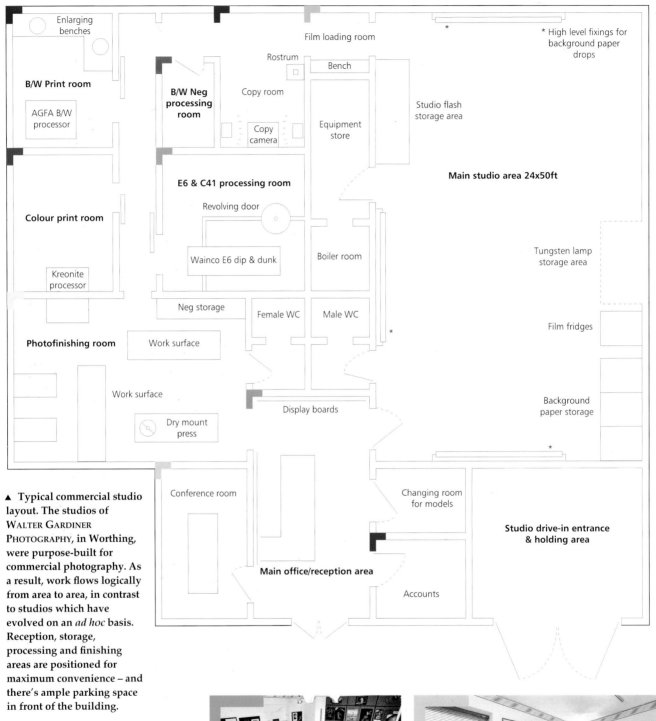

Enlarging benches

B/W Print room

AGFA B/W processor

Colour print room

Kreonite processor

Photofinishing room

Work surface

Work surface

Dry mount press

B/W Neg processing room

Copy room

Copy camera

Rostrum

Bench

E6 & C41 processing room

Revolving door

Wainco E6 dip & dunk

Neg storage

Film loading room

Equipment store

Boiler room

Female WC

Male WC

Work surface

Display boards

Studio flash storage area

Main studio area 24x50ft

Tungsten lamp storage area

Film fridges

Background paper storage

* High level fixings for background paper drops

Conference room

Main office/reception area

Changing room for models

Accounts

Studio drive-in entrance & holding area

▲ **Typical commercial studio layout.** The studios of WALTER GARDINER PHOTOGRAPHY, in Worthing, were purpose-built for commercial photography. As a result, work flows logically from area to area, in contrast to studios which have evolved on an *ad hoc* basis. Reception, storage, processing and finishing areas are positioned for maximum convenience – and there's ample parking space in front of the building.

▲ **The reception area**

▲ **Client conference room**

Tuning your studio layout to its workflow pattern – how a working studio is organised

▲ The film loading room

▲ The black-and-white printing area of the studio

▲ Copying/rostrum camera set-up

▲ Colour printing

▲ C-41 and E-6 processing

▲ Black-and-white processing

▲ All-important accounts department

▲ The photofinishing area

Managing the image

All photographers know that the statement 'the camera never lies' is, and always has been, untrue. In fact it is this precise quality that helps you to manage the image

Main light (parabolic reflector)
Blue
White
Orange
Blue
Floor light

When a client brings a box full of widgets to your studio, he's not looking for a photograph that is a straight likeness. If that's all he wanted, he could probably do it himself. He's paying you to manage the image: to make the product look interesting and perhaps stress certain benefits or convey a message such as 'our products are environmentally friendly'. Even when he does seem to want a straight likeness – say for a catalogue shot on a white background – he relies on you to show the product to its best advantage, to bring out its essence.

The extent to which you are able to manage an image, often determines your reputation as a photographer and, as a result, the kind of fees you can command. And, incidentally, it will probably ensure your survival no matter what happens in the field of image capture – digitised images, holograms, virtual reality and whatever unimagined imaging devices belong to the future. Because however sophisticated the technology gets, we shall never duplicate the creativity and originality of the human brain in finding fresh ways of seeing the things around us.

So try not to think, 'It's only a pack shot, let's bang it off'. Almost any product shot offers the potential for an original interpretation. When the great industrial photographer, Walter Nurnberg, was learning his craft in Germany in the early 1930s, he went to a large department store and borrowed a catalogue listing all the products on sale. He then worked his way through alphabetically, photographing each product in the studio, creating powerful black-and-white images on a plate camera. Whether the object was a comb, a shirt or a tube of toothpaste, he wanted to bring out its essence through careful positioning and creative lighting techniques. Photography, he felt, was a discipline that required painstaking analysis in the process of translating forms and textures into effective visual images.

Certainly this discipline, which he stressed had to be learned, served Nurnberg well when he moved over to photographing much larger objects as an industrial photographer. The techniques of lighting remained the same – you just needed bigger lamps – while what he had learned in the studio about camera angles, helped him to select the best viewpoint for a

▲ STEVE BICKNELL took this shot of 'pick and place' equipment in use, for a
corporate profile of Rediffusion Simulators. It shows the value of choosing an
unusual viewpoint and careful lighting to emphasise the main subject, in what
otherwise might have been a rather conventional picture. *(See lighting sketch opposite)*

▶ **MIKE HEMSLEY** took this shot of a group of turbine blades for Edwards High Vacuum, 'on the hoof'. Noticing that they made graphic shapes, he rearranged them slightly and added touches of orange and blue light. He used a 75mm lens on his 5x4 camera 'to get the distortion', as well as camera movements to ensure sharp focus. Notice how white light is used as well as gels, to ensure that the image is not swamped with colour.

White umbrella

Orange gel

Blue gel

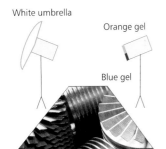

particular scene, often achieved by climbing a ladder or lying on the floor.

The most important lesson we can learn from Nurnberg's approach, is that to create a good photograph, we need to analyse the problems in translating an object into an effective visual image. And that this process of analysis remains important no matter what size the object may be. As Nurnberg suggested, this is a process that needs to be learned through practical experience. There is no easy formula. The best we can do here is to look at the problems involved and try to suggest a few broad solutions.

The problem As we discussed in the section on

lighting, human vision is very different from photography. We have already talked about 'accommodation', which is the ability of the eye and brain to average out any inconsistencies so that in effect we see what we want to see. In addition, it's worth remembering that we have two eyes which gives us binocular vision enabling us to perceive three-dimensional depth, whereas the single lens of a camera records a flat, two-dimensional image in a print or transparency. Finally, human vision is continuous, whereas the camera freezes only one instant.

Suppose you have a new car delivered. When it arrives, you walk round it admiring the various features: the flowing lines, the

◄ This is basically the same product as the shot on the opposite page, only now MIKE HEMSLEY gives this precision turbo vacuum pump the studio treatment. 'Externally,' he remembers, 'it looked more like a milk churn.' So he set about creating an 'X-ray' effect to show the casing and turbine blades in the same shot. This involved a two-stage exposure against a black background: First: The casing was cross-lit with blue and yellow filtered light, to give edge lighting only. Then: The casing was removed and the turbine blades cross-lit with blue and yellow but with frontal white light added to give detail.

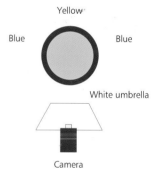

Yellow

Blue   Blue

White umbrella

Camera

colour and sheen of the paintwork, the upholstery, the dashboard, the engine – all these factors combine in giving you an impression. Now try to translate that experience into photography. Could you do it with one shot? Remember, the camera can only record one instant from a single viewpoint. So the best you could achieve is a compromise – selecting an angle which best sums up at least some of the things you feel about the car. But there are other problems too. The car is parked in front of your house – it's difficult to find a good position for your camera and the background is messy and distracting. It's late afternoon, the light is failing. None of these things mattered particularly when you were relying on your eyes. The brain isolated the car from its background and compensated for the poor light. Continuous binocular vision gave it depth and roundness of form. Messy reflections in the paintwork went unnoticed. But when they are fixed in a single photograph, all these imperfections suddenly become noticeable and distracting.

Is it surprising then, that car photographers prefer to work in the studio, where lighting, background, reflections and viewpoint can all

'If you can find a new way of looking at things, people will be interested. Everyone is desperate for new ideas.'

Peter Dazeley, advertising photographer

be carefully controlled? Not only can they produce 'cleaner' images, but the controls available enable them to manage the image in such a way that the selling points – whether they be power, luxury, economy, safety or capacity – can be underlined. The car photographer analyses the problems inherent in translating a complex, multi-faceted object into a pleasing photograph. To be successful, of course, he or she has to go much further, creating, through individual lighting techniques and composition, an image which can even exceed the expectations of the viewer, conveying in a visual form, the message which sells the car. But for the moment let's concentrate on the basics.

Viewpoint How you frame a shot has to be vital, because unlike the experience of seeing with your eyes, with photography you only get one chance. Take a look at your hand. Turn it round and study it from different angles, trying to see it as a flat shape, a two-dimensional representation. You'll notice that while to your brain it remains a hand from all angles, the two-dimensional shape only looks 'natural' in certain positions – from some viewpoints it just looks like a lump. This is why the best painters and portrait photographers pay a lot of atten-

tion to the posing of hands. In fact you can quickly spot a second-rate portraitist, just because the hands look wrong.

It's the same with almost any object you are asked to photograph. The number of viewpoints which 'work', are limited in number. You may also need to consider other factors: which angle best shows the function of the object? Which gives it the most pleasing or interesting shape? There again, with objects which may be considered commonplace, you may prefer to choose an unexpected angle which surprises the viewer.

Backgrounds Leading directly from a consideration of the object itself, is an awareness of what's behind it. Because, as we have discussed, whereas human vision is binocular and can 'read' depth, the camera records in a flat plane. This leads to the common mistake, often made by amateurs, of trees appearing to grow out of the subject's head. Unfortunately, professionals are not immune to this fault.

The problem can be overcome by simplifying the background – perhaps throwing it out of focus or, in the studio, using plain walls or paper backdrops. But it's probably more useful to see it in another way – the need to isolate the subject. In the studio this can be achieved through careful positioning, on location – say in a factory – the subject can be isolated by a combination of stage management, viewpoint and lighting. Remembering that the camera records everything; by eliminating distractions and isolating the subject, you are saying, in effect, 'This is what I want you to look at.'

Depth Now let's look at the whole picture. As we have said, any photographic representation is limited to a flat two-dimensional plane. But to achieve the sensation of depth that we enjoy with human vision, we need to create a feeling of space, an illusion of that third dimension. There are two principal ways of achieving this illusion – both of which were mastered by great painters long before photography was invented.

The first method is to control light and shade. Careful lighting gives the subject itself substance, a feeling of weight and solidity. Attention to the background and sometimes, the foreground, will further enhance this feeling of depth, through tonal separation: for example, suppose your subject is well lit in the middle-ground, then to achieve a sensation of depth, your foreground and background should be kept darker.

Secondly, the illusion of depth can be achieved through controlling perspective. In photography, we have the added advantage that apparent perspective can be exaggerated through use of wide-angle lenses and camera movements, though if a 'realistic' image is required, then care must be taken to minimise distortions. Finally, if it sounds as though we may be laying down rules, then it's important to remember that in photography what is good is what works. Sometimes it may suit our purpose for the image not to simulate a feeling of depth. Objects seen in a flat plane, perhaps shot from overhead, can create strong 'graphic' shapes or patterns, which in themselves make compelling pictures.

Colour When colour photography was first introduced on a mass scale, it wasn't difficult to sell the idea to amateurs – they were delighted at the idea of producing pictures which seemed closer to their actual experience of the world around them. For professionals, however, the business of producing coherent, meaningful pictures, was often made more difficult in colour. Unless it was carefully controlled, the presence of colour was apt to distract the viewer from the intention of the picture. In fact, some photographers still prefer to work in black-and-white, while others subdue colour to an extent that the result is almost monochrome.

So it's important to appreciate that colour is not just a means of making things look more natural or realistic. It brings with it a whole set of new considerations, which in some cases can help the photographer, but more often will create extra problems. On the positive side, colour can be used to isolate the subject: for example, a mid-tone red object will stand out starkly against a mid-tone blue or green background – an effect which does not transfer to black-and-white. From a technical point of view, the in-built contrast between different colours is very useful, because it allows the contrast ratio between bright and dark areas of an image to be kept low – within the narrow limits of colour film and effective reproduction.

On the other hand, the skillful photographer will probably spend more time co-ordinating and harmonising colours, to prevent them from distracting the viewer from the pure message of the picture. Used carefully, colour can be a powerful means towards managing the image. In the wrong hands, the result is all too often something cheap and garish.

Composition Finally, let's pull all these elements together and decide what it is that makes a good picture. As we've discussed, human vision is highly selective and accommodating: it sorts out the mess around us and sees what it wants to see. Obviously the camera cannot do this, so the photographer has to help – either by selecting the right viewpoint or by moving objects around. This is composition.

Over the years, teachers and writers have devised many rules to try to explain how good composition works. In practical terms, composition - a sense of design - is something you

have to discover for yourself, both through your own work and by seeing what's good in the work of others. A good place to begin is that all good design starts with simplification.

When you look critically at the layout of a newspaper or magazine, you'll notice that the most important task of the designer is sort out the jumble of information, labelling the different parts of the page clearly and presenting them in a form that is easy to follow. Once clarity is achieved, the designer may take things a step further, looking at the shape of the page, using pictures and type to underline the message, or to produce a layout that is surprising, dramatic or beautiful in itself. Designing a photograph follows exactly the same process. Your first task is to simplify – to sort out the jumble. This is done by making sure the main subject is rendered clearly and by eliminating or subordinating everything that might be distracting. Once you've done that, you can concentrate on making a beautiful picture: seeing the shapes and how they work together.

Remember the famous Benson & Hedges advertisements? The ideas and the effect they produced may have been weird and intriguing, but the pictures themselves were very simple. Each element was clearly readable – beautifully lit, composed and colour coordinated. When your business is communication, clarity is all.

▲ Another beautiful shot by TESSA TRAEGER, this time showing the importance of backgrounds. Here Traeger's choice of pink tissue paper is inspired. Not only does the tissue complement the colour of the garlic so that the picture is almost monochromatic (pink/white), but it also echoes the flimsy texture of the garlic skins.

He who pays the piper, calls the tune, goes the saying. All well and good when the client knows exactly what he wants from an assignment and puts it on paper. But often you'll find yourself calling the tune as well as playing it – and then hoping that the piper gets paid...

Assignments

Photograph: Christopher Joyce

Brief
The business of commercial photography invariably involves working to a brief. There should be no underestimating the importance of nailing down the details...
encounter

In commercial photography the vast majority of jobs begin with a brief. And if you find yourself starting a job without a brief, then the best policy is to get one at once – even if it's just a question of writing to your client along the lines: 'This is to confirm my understanding of our discussion... etc'. Because without a brief – preferably in writing – you will be on very shaky ground if the client decides he doesn't like what you do, or that you haven't done what he asked. Of course, you may have such a good relationship with the client that he just calls you and asks you to do so and so. But even then, it doesn't hurt to drop him a line confirming the job, what is expected of you and the fees, including expenses, that may be involved.

A brief or commission is a legal contract: an agreement between two parties to provide certain services and materials in return for payment. So the clearer the wording, the better you (and the client for that matter) are protected in case of disagreement. Apart from legal considerations, a good brief will also help you get it absolutely clear what the job involves technically and creatively, and how the client

sees it. And if, as sometimes happens, the client is vague about requirements, then following a detailed discussion, it will certainly help to put something down in writing.

Basically photographic briefs fall into two categories: we could call them 'open' and 'closed'. The closed brief will be familiar to many photographers working in the general commercial and advertising fields. It typically consists of a layout or 'visual', which is usually the work of an art director or layout artist. Sometimes these visuals can be very elaborate, using magic marker pens to show all the colours and lighting effects – though some designers have difficulty getting photographic perspective spot on! Since this represents the idea which has been 'sold' to the client, there's often little room for modification or improvement. In this case the job of the photographer is to translate the visual idea into a workable photograph. This may involve considerable skill and technical inventiveness, but if the translation is accurate, the photographer wins approval. After all, the art director is only human and will certainly be gratified and flattered to see his or her idea translated faithfully

the feeling you get when you finally find a PC to satisfy your thirst for computing power without rching your bank balance.

into a high quality photograph. And a happy client leads to more work...

Many photographers feel more at home with a closed brief, because once you've cracked it, there's no argument. Others prefer the freedom and challenge of a more open brief, for example: 'Here's the product, see what you can do with it...' But in cases like this the experienced photographer will want to find out more. What are the product's selling points or benefits? What type of person is likely to use the product? How will the photograph be used? This is important because different treatments are appropriate for press releases, magazine covers, brochures or advertising applications. For example there's not much point in making an elaborate, creative shot full of coloured lights or image manipulation, if the intended use is a product release for business or technical magazines. What the editor wants is something clean and clearly lit, which shows what the product looks like, perhaps on a white background to make cutouts easier. On the other hand, if the editor is looking for a cover shot, then a creative, eye-catching picture may be exactly what fits the bill.

Creative freedom may be enjoyable for the photographer, but for the client it can be a headache. The balance is delicate. When the client gives the photographer an open brief, of course he or she hopes to be surprised and delighted by an eye-catching, creative solution.

But there's also a need to for clear communication of a particular message – usually to the client's customers. And sometimes over-creative photography can obscure the clarity of this message. Photography is a powerful medium, but it works best when it's kept elegantly simple. When working to an open brief, once they have devised an effective treatment, the best photographers then pare down the picture to its bare essentials, so that nothing distracts from the central idea.

Too much freedom can be dangerous. Which is perhaps why, in commercial photography, much of the best work comes from creative collaboration – a sort of compromise between open and closed briefs. Often this partnership is between photographer and art director or designer, though it can be equally effective with a client who has had no formal design training, but is used to dealing with photographers. The important factor is to work with someone who has no direct involvement in the photographic process. This leaves them free to read photographs or visual ideas purely in terms of communication: have we got there? Does the picture work? What does it say to me?

To anyone with an eye on the business side of photography – making money – all this may seem a bit arty. But finding the best creative solutions makes sense in business terms too. After all, if your pictures work, then so will you!

▲ On some assignments, speed is of the essence. This 96-sheet poster for Acclaim video games (art directed by John Carver of the Leisure Group) was up in 50 prime London sites just eight days after PETER DAZELEY started shooting the pictures. Here's the timetable:

Friday 1.00pm: Dazeley receives layout by fax;
Friday 5.00pm: commissioned for job;
Monday 10.30am: starts shooting basketball pictures;
Tuesday 3.30am: pictures finished (a long session!);
Wednesday pm: after manipulation on Barco Creator, final composite of transparencies ready;
Following Tuesday: posters in position.

In themselves, computers are not visually exciting. It's up to art directors and photographers to create imaginative ideas suggesting what computers can do, rather than what they look like. So when art director Piotr Henning, of the Matthew Poppy agency, dreampt up this visual for Elonex, it was up to advertising photographer PETER DAZELEY to find a solution that didn't involve a trip to the Sahara desert. With a little help from the Quantel Paintbox at Tapestry (extra sand dunes and so on in middle distance), the whole thing was

▲ Piotr Henning's original layout

▶ A boxed platform holds the sand and key props, as Dazeley's assistant adds water to the screen casing. The snooted spotlight will bounce blue light onto the screen from coloured reflectors on floor (see next picture).

▶ With the model in place, excess water is dried off the screen casing before another shot is taken. The palm leaf is used to achieve a ribbed effect on the sand, it will not appear in the final image.

▲ The final effect. This picture crops down into something very close to the final image. Several versions were shot because of the unpredictability of splashed water and to make sure that the model's expression was right.

◄ The finished advertisement, showing the added sand dunes and how the copy worked with the finished composite image.

MICHAEL ST MAUR SHEIL specialises in corporate photography. In his line of work, a single assignment can last 73 days, involving 38 different flights and 500 rolls of film. Unlike some of his colleagues, however, he prefers to travel light, restricting camera gear to medium format or 35mm with no more than two portable flash guns. This suits his style which is close to photo reportage: 'I photograph what I see,' he states simply.

These pictures are from an annual report for the Costain Group. As on most of Sheil's assignments the brief was loose – little more than a list of locations. The decision to use black and white came from The Partners, who designed the report.

▲ Unusually, for this picture of giant 12-metre sewage pipes in Athens, Sheil employed a little stage management. After climbing up the lattice of a crane to get the high angle, he asked the workman to stand in the right spot to add a sense of scale.

▲ When Sheil arrived at this construction site on the M4 motorway in Wales, he had expected to be photographing a spectacular completed section. But, as is often the way, nothing was ready and the weather was atrocious with very poor visibility. So he asked the site foreman to show him round and then got on with it. This striking low level shot was unposed.

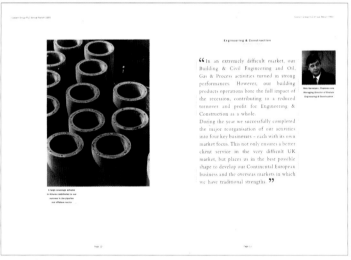

► In this shot of an open-cut coal mine in East Kentucky, the mechanical digger is almost incidental. In order to tell the story, Sheil felt it was important to give a powerful sense of the environment.

Architectural photographer JULIAN NIEMAN has done many assignments for Country Life *magazine. Although he has used large format and still does occasionally, because of the pressure to 'get more shots done in a day', Nieman tends to shoot this type of work on small format cameras, using shift lenses where necessary. This assignment, to photograph Hoare's Bank in Fleet Street, London, was fairly typical. The writer, Richard Haslam, visited the bank first, producing a shot list for Nieman together with notes on suggested viewpoints, security procedures and useful contacts. Since budgets on magazines are limited, one day was allowed for around a dozen pictures, including exteriors, interiors, 'still life' details and paintings.*

On this occasion, writer RICHARD HASLAM also produced reference shots to show Nieman what he was after. Shown alongside (and smaller than) Nieman's pictures, they provide a neat illustration of the photographer's contribution to the project.

▶ **The cashiers' hall: with a better viewpoint and use of a solitary figure; note how Nieman has increased the sense of space and grandeur.**

▶ **The museum: Nieman takes a wider angle view to increase the sense of depth and include the chandelier.**

▲ The drawing room: by changing the viewpoint, Nieman cuts out those distracting light-coloured chairs, gets the chandelier in and makes better use of the mirror reflection to increase the feeling of depth.

▲ The dining room: a better angle and obviously it helped that they had finished laying the table by the time Nieman arrived!

▲ Sir Richard Hoare as Lord Mayor of London in 1745: naturally, Nieman uses cross lighting rather than camera-mounted flash for this painting.

Freestyle: When you get the rare chance to 'do your own thing' it's a great opportunity to make your mark in style

Imagine an assignment where the client, a leading advertising agency, offers you a large amount of money and says, 'Just go out to these locations and shoot whatever you like...' Certainly it doesn't happen every day, and when it does, the agency needs a photographer who it believes will deliver the goods. Such a photographer is CHRISTOPHER JOYCE who, since the early 1960s, has built up a strong enough reputation from his advertising work to earn this kind of trust. The project, for Charterhouse Bank, involved three leading photographers from Britain, France and Germany. For the UK segment, Joyce was given 10 days, during which time he exposed 66 rolls of 35mm black and white film, from which 31 images were finally chosen. These were used in an exhibition, a book, a calendar and a corporate advertising campaign. So you could say that the agency, DMB&B, got their money's worth!

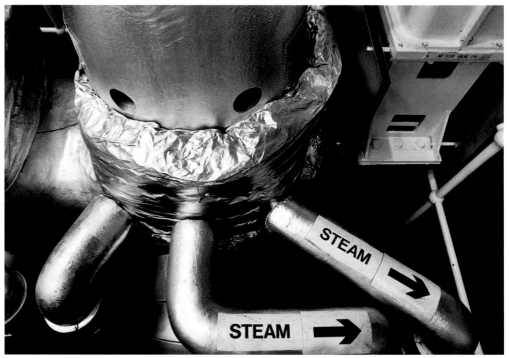

All photographs: Christopher Joyce

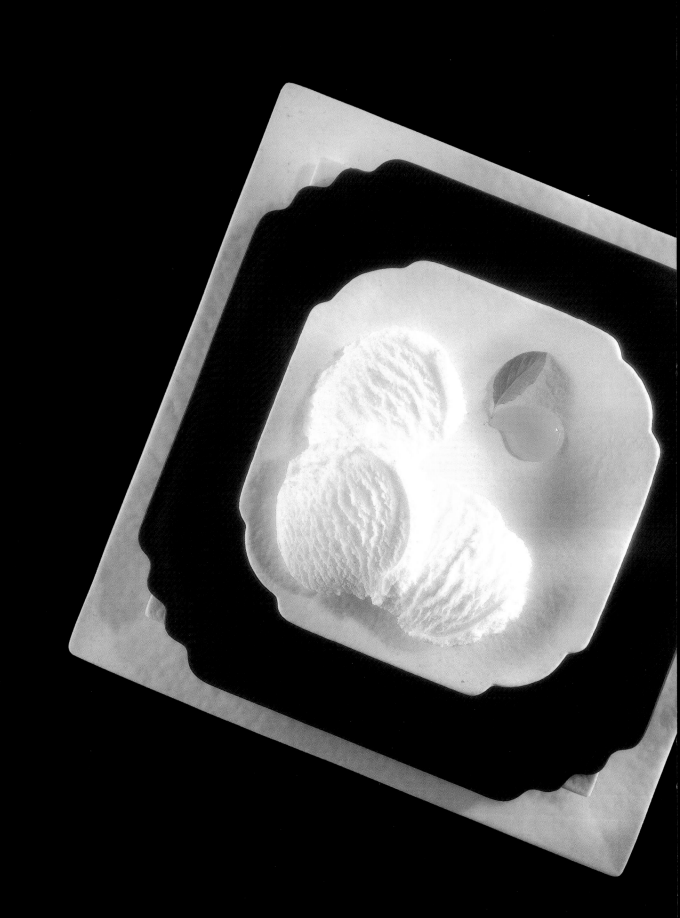

Product
photography

Product photography is a major
earner for most commercial studios.
It can be glamorous and creative, but
more often than not what is required
is an accurate, high quality record of a
particular product. Anything more
elaborate is usually precluded by
time, budgets and the actual purpose
of the picture. A prime requirement is
the ability to solve problems quickly
and elegantly – as with this ice cream
shot by Paul Webster where the
product is liable to melt!

Problem
solving

Whatever else you may feel about your business, you are there to provide a service. And like most service companies your role is to solve someone's problem. Forget problems, concentrate on the solutions

You're just about to pack up for the day when the telephone rings. It's your favourite design agency: 'We're just finishing the mock-ups for that new pack design for XYZ perfume company, can we bike them over when they're ready? We need prints for a presentation tomorrow morning...' Or perhaps it's your local PR agency wanting product pictures for a rush press release. One thing you can be sure of: the pictures are needed in a hurry.

Product photography is usually the bread-and-butter work of a commercial studio. At first sight, it often seems that little creativity is involved – especially when you're given so little time to think about the picture. This causes some photographers to feel that so-called 'pack shots' are slightly beneath them. This is a dangerous attitude because on the one hand it may lead to sloppy

▲ This pack shot for Guinness by Jᴏɴ Lɪᴘᴘᴇᴛ was trickier to achieve than it might appear. As jewellery photographers know, metallic gold is one of the most difficult surfaces to render in a 'lifelike' manner. Lippet used an angled overhead lightbox slightly forward of the cans, placed against a white background, and two curved white reflectors on either side of his 5x4 camera. He then needed to use rising front on the camera to retain the verticals as well as the gold reflection.

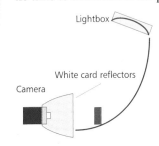

◄ For this perfume shot, MIKE HEMSLEY wanted highly directional lighting. He used a 500W tungsten spotlight, with dulling spray on the bottles to diffuse the image. To achieve a mixture of sharpness and soft focus, half the exposure (10 seconds at f/22) was taken normally and the other half shot through a polythene bag. A small, cut-out white card reflector was used just behind the bottle to make it 'glow'.

Reflector

Camera

photography, on the other, to a wish to introduce more creativity by 'jazzing up' the picture with lighting effects, props or fancy backgrounds. Sometimes this may be appropriate, but when a straightforward record of the product is all that was required, the net result may be to irritate the client.

In fact, rendering a three-dimensional object faithfully and realistically in a two-dimensional picture, can require a great deal of creativity. And it may be that a failure to realise this is the main reason why so much work of this type is second rate. In product photography the first duty of the photographer is to the product itself: its shape, its surface texture, its colour, its purpose and so on. Each quality of a product poses different problems – in lighting, composition, camera movements, backgrounds and host of other considerations. The skill of a photographer can be said to be the measure of his or her ability to solve these problems.

With studio-based photographers, this accounts for the popularity of large banks of electronic flash heads housed in a rectangular box covered with a translucent diffusing material – sometimes known as 'light boxes' or 'softboxes'. These units – available in many shapes and sizes – give a soft, even, diffused light,

▶ **Another product shot by** JON LIPPET. **Lighting set-up is similar to the Guinness cans picture only this time Lippet used a 'flag' just above the pack to reduce the highlight. Again, precise exposure was required to 'hold' the black lever at the top, against the dark background.**

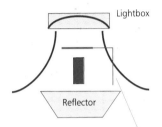

Lightbox

Reflector

Flag to reduce highlight on top of pack

with a low contrast ratio which is good for reproduction. An added advantage is that their square shape produces clean white reflections. For simple product shots, they are also quick and simple to use as a main light, producing good professional quality with only a single reflector to 'fill in' the shadow areas.

It could be argued that the popularity of this lighting set-up leads to bland photography, lacking in variety and excitement. However, from the client's point of view, with this type of job, seeing the product clearly is more important than fancy lighting effects. So unless you feel very confident of your lighting techniques, it's usually better to stick to a formula that works and can be done quickly and efficiently (remember: time is money). Moreover, using

the soft box as a basic main light set-up, it's also possible to refine the technique by adding other lights, usually snooted for greater directional accuracy, to pick out particular features of the product.

As we said earlier, product photography is about solving problems. So let's try to analyse some of the problems you are likely to encounter. With experienced photographers, this thought process usually becomes second nature like reading or writing, so that they are scarcely aware why they decide to photograph certain objects in a particular way. Here are some points they are likely to consider:

Purpose It goes without saying that before you start it's vital to establish the purpose, or even-

Side lights

Bare bulbs

tual destination, of the picture. Not only will this dictate the treatment you give it, but also the time you spend and hence, how much you charge. For example, enhancing an image to the level where it might be accepted as a magazine or brochure cover, will take much more time and thought than a straight picture for a press release. Even when, as can be the case with manufacturers or distributors, the purpose of the picture is not yet decided, you need to establish the most likely uses. For example, is the image likely to be cut out for use in a catalogue? If so a shadowless white background will obviously make more sense than a dark colour. On the other hand, when the purpose is not clear and you can spare the time, then it may pay you to give the product a more creative treatment as well as providing a straight record shot. But bear in mind that the most common requirements are speed, service and high technical standards.

Surface As we all know, photography works by recording on film the light reflected from the subject. But the manner in which that light is reflected, absorbed, diffused or scattered can vary enormously - hence the importance of looking closely at the surface of an object. Here are some of the surfaces you are likely to encounter:
• Dark matt surfaces absorb light rather than reflecting it back into the camera. For example, black cameras can be tricky to photograph because, not surprisingly, the manufacturer wants to see all the control levers, dials and knobs with absolute clarity, even though they may be black on black. Hence calculating the right exposure can be tricky and box light set-

▶ When STEVE BICKNELL was asked to photograph the range of test tube racks shown opposite, he worked hard to create something interesting from a collection of 'uninspiring' products. In final version of the original shot, a large transparent test tube was double exposed over this strong, geometric background. Here, he recreates the steps he went through to arrive at the background picture.

▲ Preparation: 'I start by studying the basic elements of the product before deciding on a direction for the picture. In this case, the most obvious feature of the racks is their regularity of shape and material...'

ups will usually need to be supplemented with narrow, directional beams and reflectors to pick out details.

• Light matt surfaces give rise to the opposite problem – detail lost in highlights rather than shadow areas. This calls for careful lighting and contrast control, allowing enough shadow area to give the object bulk, while retaining the feeling of its light colour. Sometimes a 'high key' lighting approach, may be effective.

• Textured surfaces – fabrics for example – usually require a direct, angled light to bring them into relief. As with all these lighting problems, experimentation – playing with the lights – and trusting what you see, will generally give you the required result.

• Metallic and other reflective surfaces can cause all sorts of problems. With mirror-like surfaces – a silver teapot for example – it will be necessary to construct a 'light tent' of translucent material around the object allowing a small aperture for the camera lens, to prevent camera and photographer appearing in the picture. More general problems are caused by reflection of lights. In this respect, rectangular soft boxes produce clean reflections, whereas flash umbrellas look unnatural. When lighting reflective objects such as cars, the real secret is to light not the subject but the area around it – background

▲ Composition: 'To avoid any distraction, I chose a black background. This also allowed me to place the products at different levels to create a feeling of space and depth. To add to the sense of perspective, I used a semi-wide 115mm lens on the 5x4 camera.'

walls, large reflector boards and so on. Sometimes when a particular reflection seems impossible to avoid, a dulling spray can be used to reduce it, but this should be used sparingly.

• Glass and other see-through materials give the photographer two sets of problems. Firstly their translucency needs to be conveyed and secondly, they tend to be reflective as well. Here again experimentation is the key. Only you can decide the exact placement of lights and reflectors for a particular bottle or glass. However, as a general principle, translucency is best conveyed with reflectors. With a light coloured background this entails lighting the background in such a way as to reflect light back through the object. With dark backgrounds, it will be necessary to cut the reflector to an exact size so that it is hidden behind the object and angled to catch the light.

Shape Study the object carefully to establish the best angle for your picture. Since photographs are limited to two dimensions, it may help to close one eye to reduce the illusion of depth. You should be looking for two things. Firstly, what angle shows off the product and its functions in the most realistic and informative manner? Secondly, what makes the most pleasing shape? Fortunately, these two demands often coincide. Obviously, viewpoint must also be considered: for example, shooting

▲ Lighting: 'Photographers often try to light every element of a product, but this can produce dull pictures – shadows are just as important as highlights... The main light was a large grid, angled to reflect directly off the surface of the racks; two strips of gold gel were placed over this light to add warmth. Overhead is an 'effect light' with strong blue gel and parabolic reflector to keep it contained: this fills in the shadows and adds depth, though it's important not to overlight shadow areas, just fill enough to give detail. Finally two other snooted lights were placed on either side of the upright rack at the back to break up the solid blue fill in.'

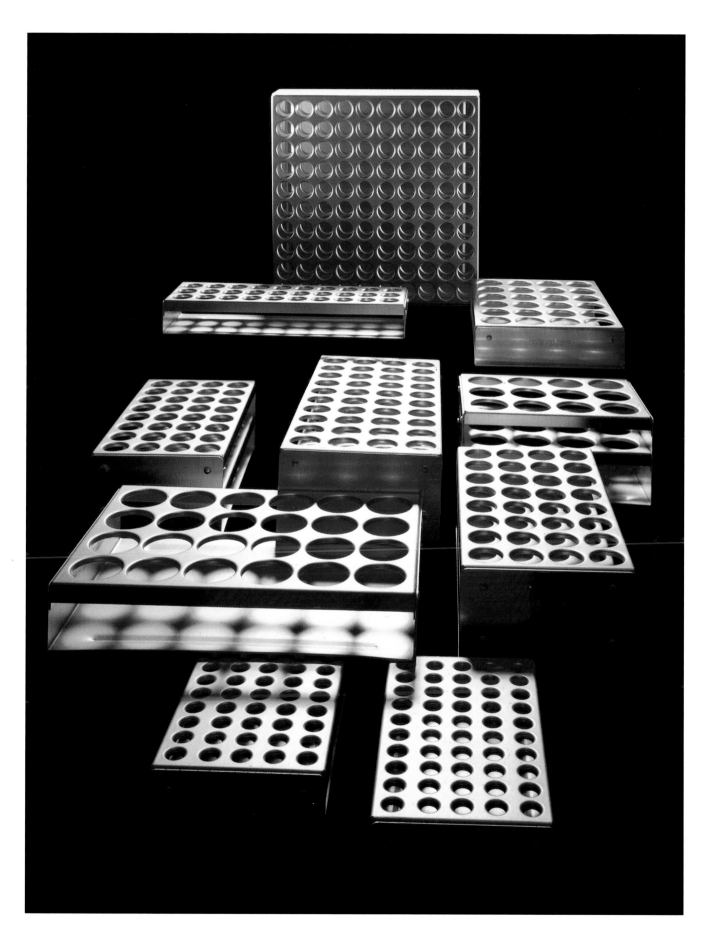

Photocomposition

▶ *To add excitement to this product shot of a circuit board, MIKE HEMSLEY of Walter Gardiner Photography, enlisted the help of a vacuum cleaner! This is how the photocomposition was done in three separate stages on the rostrum camera. All material was taped to a pin registered strip of film to ensure that each element was kept in registration. Some photographers might have preferred to use digital imaging to combine the elements, but Hemsley reckons he can save his clients money and produce equally convincing results using conventional photocomposition.*

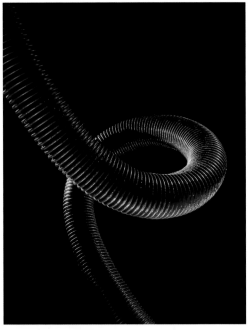

● **Stage 1: Image 1 (the hose of a vacuum cleaner) is combined with Mask 5 (a lith shot of the circuit board). At each stage a diffuser is placed between the two of them to create soft masking.**

● **Stage 2: Image 2 is combined with Mask 5, with dialled-in dichroic colours beneath various highlight areas.**

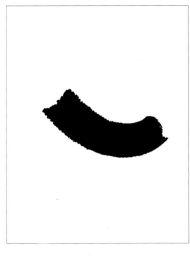

● **Stage 3: Image 4 is combined with Mask 3. The final composite image is shown opposite**

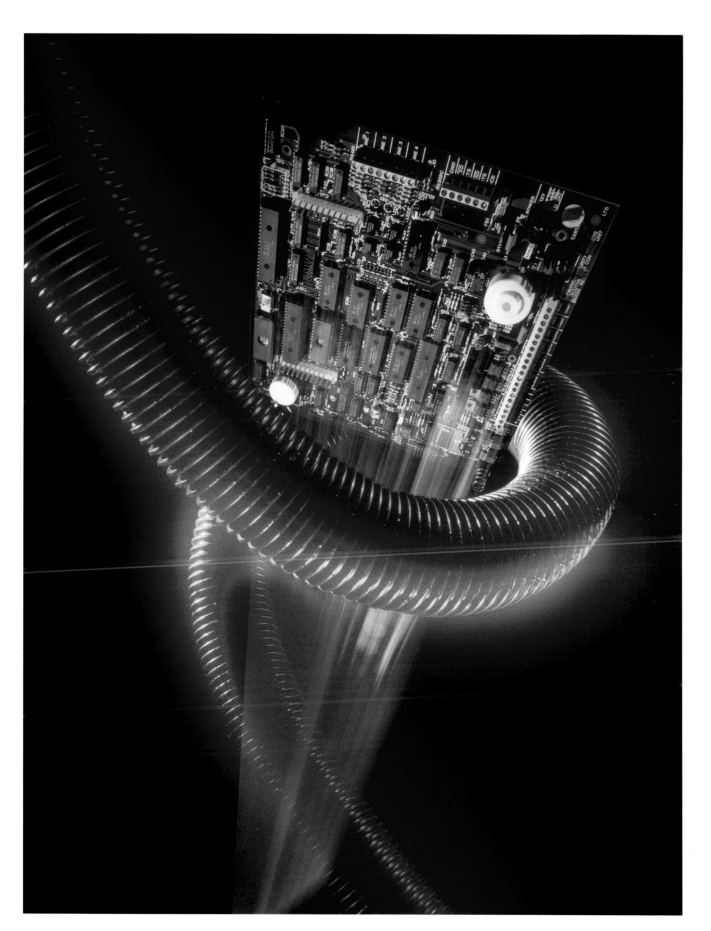

▲ PAUL WEBSTER specialises in ice cream photography. This shot and the image introducing this section were taken from an assignment to shoot the complete range of Safeway ice creams – both show Safeway white Italian ice cream. The secret, he says, is to work quickly, and use a food stylist or home economist – in this case, Elaine Bastable. He never uses fake material and you'd be surprised how difficult it is to achieve a perfect looking 'scoop' using real ice cream! Notice how tightly Webster controls the plane of focus to emphasise the ice cream in this 10x8 transparency.

a food can from a very low angle would make it look more like a towering building – this might add interest and impact but would it be appropriate? Sometimes shapes can be exaggerated by using perspective-distorting wide angle lenses. This technique may be useful for adding visual impact to box-shaped products, but again, sympathy for the actual shape of the product should be preserved as far as possible.

Colour The importance of colour depends on the product. On the one hand, a metallic engineering component or grey computer casing, may need livening up with some coloured light. Here the best technique is to keep the main light white and put colour gels on supplementary lights, perhaps lighting only the rim of the object with coloured light. With smaller, dull coloured objects, it may be sufficient to warm them up a little by using gold or coloured reflectors. At the other end of the scale, products such as food, clothing or labels on cans and packaging, demand faithful and accurate colour rendering. This can only be achieved by careful testing of film materials, processing and the colour temperature of your lights. Remember that coloured backgrounds can also produce unwanted colour casts.

Functionality Finally, we also need to consider the use of the product. Obviously, a nut cracker will look more realistic with a broken nut beside it. But other demonstrations of function may require prior discussion with the client.

For example, a lawn mower could be photographed in the studio as a straight product shot, or it could be pictured in action on a lawn, perhaps involving model hire, more time and greater expense. Using models will add to the cost of the shot but can pay dividends in creating greater realism. On the other hand, a few judiciously chosen props may be sufficient to suggest the use of the product, earning the thanks of your client for saving time and money.

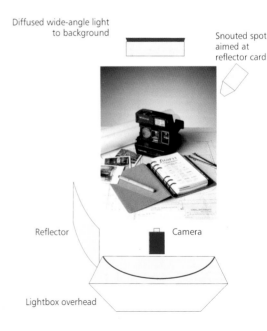

Diffused wide-angle light to background

Snouted spot aimed at reflector card

Reflector

Camera

Lightbox overhead

▲ An 'application' product shot for Polaroid, by JON LIPPET, suggesting possible use by an architect. Three light sources were used. A snooted spot was directed onto a reflector which pushes light into the dark camera. For overall clarity, a diffused lightbox was placed overhead. Finally, a diffused wideangle lamp creates the soft glow on the mid-tone grey background behind the camera. *(See facing diagram)*

Industrial
& Corporate

As the face of industry changes, the traditional image of industrial photography is changing too. Today's specialists are likely to be photographing electronic components or computer screens rather than steel mills or shipbuilding. And they are likely to refer to themselves as 'corporate' rather than 'industrial' photographers...

Photograph: Danny Maddocks for British Gas.

Images of industry

Like graphic design, photography is all about communication. And when it comes to industrial (or what is now often called corporate) photography there are many important messages to get across

▲ A beautifully balanced exposure adds drama to this dusk shot of a cement works for an ARC annual report, by Peter Lowry. Night shots can be a useful option for exteriors in corporate/industrial work and they are less dependent on good weather conditions.

Once upon a time, industrial companies were defined by their activities: mining, metal smelting, chemical processing, manufacturing, shipbuilding, heavy construction and so on. What's more, they wanted to be recognised by pictures of the processes that were central to their business – hence the traditional image of 'industrial photography': heavy machinery, blast furnaces, huge construction sites – all suggesting the power and success of the company.

These days things are rather different. For a start, many of these heavy industries are no longer with us, and have been replaced by lighter 'hi-tech' electronics businesses. But even those heavyweights which remain usually prefer to be seen as clean, modern, and highly computerised. Images which hark back to the power and brutality of the Industrial Revolution tend to be seen as old-fashioned and, perhaps, even slightly distasteful. Today the stress is on computerised controls, clean operations, the environment and human values.

As for the photographers, they now regard themselves as 'corporate' rather than 'industrial' specialists. In some ways, the new term makes more sense and gives the photographer a wider scope. Corporate – as in 'corporate identity', 'corporate PR', 'corporate advertising' and so on – implies the face that a company wants to present to its public. In this respect, the task is more general than that of product or service advertising – even though the way consumers perceive a company's products can be seen as part of that company's corporate image.

Here are some typical corporate messages a company might wish to convey:
• We are a highly successful company, showing continuous growth
• We are an efficient company
• We are a quality-conscious company
• We are a company that cares about its customers

◄ A picture may be worth a thousand words but are they the right words? IAN MCKINNELL was pleased with this shot of Princes Quay Shopping Centre, Hull, for Land Securities annual report. Fireworks are tricky and unpredictable: after carefully positioning his camera, McKinnell needed 20 shots to produce this one image – exposure was eight seconds. In the event, however, the company decided not to use the picture because, in difficult times, it was felt to give the wrong signals to shareholders.

► Newcastle-based DANNY MADDOCKS of Image Photographic Services, continues to uphold the traditional values and drama of industrial photography. His lighting is always highly directional, isolating the subject and activity from its background, much in the way that the great industrial specialist of the 1950s, Walter Nurnberg, used to – only Maddocks uses snooted flash rather than tungsten spotlights. To cut out distracting elements behind the subject, he also brings plenty of black velvet. Gels are used to add colour to drab subjects, though Maddocks is careful not to overdo it, keeping skin tones, for example, as natural as possible. Preparation, Maddocks feels, is important – before photographing a plant he'll usually try to do a recce the week before, often shooting rough 35mm shots to discuss with the client. Since safety practices are a prime consideration, he also packs clean overalls, hard hats, safety glasses and ear plugs, for workers who may have 'forgotten' them.

Above • Drums Ltd
Top • Thorn Lighting

• Drums Ltd

Left • Weldex
Below • Drums Ltd

• Thorn Lighting

• We are concerned about the effects of our manufacturing processes on the environment
• We are a company worth investing in

The importance of investment helps to explain why companies are prepared to allocate large budgets for producing company reports and brochures. Often such publications may have relatively small print runs but, targeted at the right people, can prove very cost-effective.

The client For the most part, companies involved in corporate promotions, tend to be large – with international corporations often producing several special publications telling people about themselves and their activities, as well as the annual report. Smaller companies tend to concentrate on selling products, though if they are successful, they may decide to take a corporate stance as well.

In the past, it was mainly production companies which published illustrated accounts of their activities. Today, service companies are also part of this sector. So, the corporate photographer may well be working for banks, insurance companies or large accountancy firms, as well as oil companies and manufacturers. Contact may be direct with the company concerned, though more often it comes through a design company. Either way, what appeals to most photographers in this field is that briefs tend to be much looser than those for sales or product advertising work. This is because the message to be conveyed is much less precise. In company reports, for example, images are intended to make the reader feel good about the company and at the same time, brighten up a page of text or accounts.

Typically, the photographer may be asked to visit various plants or offices, taking shots of any key processes and important personnel. Beyond that, the brief is simply to bring back visually arresting pictures. Sometimes a loose theme may be suggested, such as 'people at work', and designers may have their own style theme – such as shooting the report in black and white. More often the photographer will have been chosen because his or her particular style, appeals to the designer.

Methods Traditionally, industrial photography involved heavy equipment – nearly

Fermentation unit

1.5k unit with yellow gel

0.5k unit coned down onto face as modest fill-in

▶ When NORMAN CHILDS arrived at APSEL Ltd to take this picture, the product he was supposed to photograph wasn't ready. So, after consultation with the client, this shot of the fermentation unit was 'dummied up' with a little yellow light added to help the picture along.

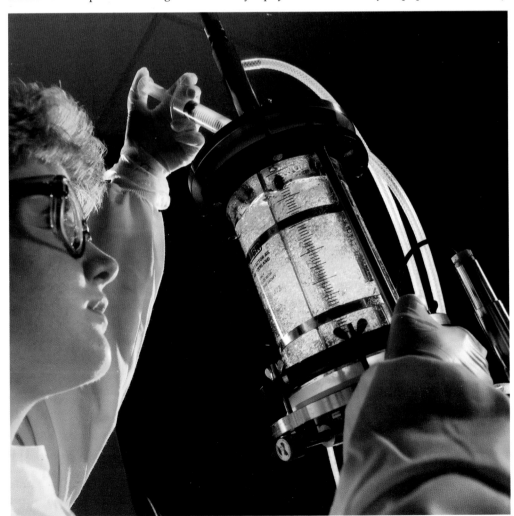

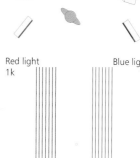

◀ This graphic arrangement of a stack of nuclear fuel rods framing the subject, was created almost from nothing. NORMAN CHILDS noticed the pile of rods and had them built up especially for the picture. Blue and red gels add a little excitement, but notice how Childs keeps the coloured lights off the workman, lighting him with white light, coned down to prevent light spread causing any dilution of the coloured lights.

Nuclear fuel rods

1k units on man coned down to prevent light spread

Red light
1k

Blue light
1k

Stacks of fuel rods positioned in front of the camera

always large format cameras – and masses of lighting gear. But though some specialists still operate in this manner, others have found success travelling light with portable flash guns and even – whatever next? – 35mm cameras. In the hands of skilled photographers, this represents not so much a decline in professional standards as a shift in visual emphasis.

Large format and heavy lighting are the perfect tools for showing the scale of industry – particularly interiors. How else can a large factory or foundry, for example, be lit and recorded accurately? However, smaller formats and portable flash, come into their own when the requirement is for pictures of individual workers and specific processes. The image may be less heroic, but in its way, is just as representative.

When it comes to travelling, portable equipment has definite advantages. Not only are baggage costs greatly reduced, but if the pho-

tographer can carry his own gear, then an assistant is not needed. Lighter equipment also means less intrusion into the daily schedule of the plant or office being photographed: often

'It's often a question of making silk purses out of sows' ears...'

Norman Childs, industrial photographer

an asset when cooperation on the ground is needed. Finally, with multi-site, international assignments, the potential cost savings in time and transportation, not to mention capital investment, are very large.

But whichever approach is adopted, certain requirements remain the same. Planning needs to be of the highest order, particularly in situations where communication from head office to local sites, may be unreliable. Indeed, the most difficult part may be getting to and organising the shot, rather than actually taking it. This is why most location photographers do so much

▶ A familiar London landmark, St Paul's Cathedral, by aerial specialist PAUL PROCTOR, a director of Chorley and Handford, based in Wallington, Surrey. Over the year, Proctor averages around 400 hours flying time, usually in a fixed-wing Cessna 182 with long range tanks, but occasionally in helicopters, which are much more expensive to hire but useful for low level shots over London, for example. Medium format cameras are preferred with standard or slightly longer lenses and colour film around ISO 100. 'If you feel you need a longer lens,' says Proctor, 'ask the pilot to go in closer!' His company has built up a leading reputation for aerial work throughout the UK, with clients coming from the construction industry, local councils, harbour and highway authorities, and utility companies like Nuclear Electric and National Grid. C & H maintains an extensive library and stock orders are good

of their work away from the camera: they are good at making things happen. At different times, this may mean being firm but diplomatic with local managers or generating the right kind of teamwork and enthusiasm with people on the shop floor. Photography has a certain built-in glamour, so people are usually happy to get involved, but such cooperation and goodwill can be stretched if there's too much hanging around...

Once on site, there are other requirements too. An efficient company will generally operate clean, safety-conscious sites, but there are obviously exceptions. With careful use of lighting and camera positions, it's usually possible to 'hide' untidy areas or distracting backgrounds. In any case, isolating the subject through lighting or differential focus, usually produces stronger, more meaningful pictures.

Design As we have discussed, the brief for corporate photography is usually much looser than for the product-orientated commercial assignment. In the design area, this can make things difficult, but the good designer will relish the chance to work with a varied assortment of images.

For the photographer, the key is to provide a wide range of high quality pictures, covering as many aspects as possible of each site. Sometimes details are given as to what processes must be covered, but often the brief is very loose along such lines as, 'We need at least four good shots from each location.' Beyond that, the diligent photographer will provide further options, such as scenic shots to help establish the location (hills, rivers, local people and so on), and any 'graphic' patterns (piles of components, pipes etc) which happen to catch the eye.

The need to get good pictures may sometimes conflict with what the site manager or technical personnel think should be recorded. Sometimes key aspects of an operation may be visually boring, so that while these pictures need to be taken, the photographer should bear in mind that what the designer needs is visual excitement. In the final publication, a good designer may often use, not the conventional view as suggested by the local manager, but an off-beat treatment or unusual angle which sums up an operation with graphic simplicity.

Finally, it pays to take an interest in how your pictures are used on the page. Not only does this show the designer that you care about your pictures, you may also gain valuable insights which could help you on your next assignment. The corporate photographer is above all, an illustrator, and that means that unless his or her pictures work on the page, they have failed. Not all designers know how to bring out the best in photographs – some may need tactful encouragement and enthusiasm to point them in the right direction. It is your reputation – not just the designer's – that is at stake.

◄ By contrast, GRAHAME AUSTIN of Kitchenham, Bournemouth, is a 'GP' photographer – weddings on Saturdays, portraits and commercial work during the week. Nevertheless, he manages to fit in a good deal of aerial work in the West Country area, maintaining that the secrets of success are local knowledge and good flight planning (grouping together as many clients as possible for each flight). Tourism pictures like this shot, left, of Sandbanks, Poole, sell well, as do progress shots, below, for the construction industry. Two more pieces of advice: insist on a pilot who has worked with photographers before, and if the light is bad, cancel your trip. Clear sunlight produces the best pictures.

Imagine a studio where someone else decides when to put the lights on and what power to use. Architectural photography is a bit like that. Everything depends on the light. Interior work, of course, is easier to control – though existing lighting and sheer space can also cause problems. Outside, the weather has the last word. Specialist Ian McKinnell needed direct sunlight to get this stunning shot of the Vitra Design Museum in Germany for Blueprint magazine; over four days, the sun shone for about ten minutes. He used a polarising filter to darken the sky. Architecture

Inside or out?

▶ Floodlit buildings are a godsend: they look dramatic and can be a valuable fall-back when daylight weather is poor. But it helps to catch them while there's still some light left in the sky. IAN MCKINNELL took this shot of Mobil House, London, for Land Securities' annual report.

The traditional image of an architectural photographer is a chap with a big plate camera (lots of movements) and heavy tripod, standing around outside a building waiting for the weather to improve. The reality today is that there's still a lot of waiting around and large format cameras remain the ideal format, but there have been changes.

For a start, large format monorail and view cameras no longer have the monopoly on camera movements: lens movements are now available on certain medium format models, while tilt and shift lenses can also be bought (not cheaply) for some 35mm brands. This has lead to a new breed of photographer zapping around with lightweight cameras, sometimes even – to the dismay of the purists – shooting wide-angle views of buildings which actually exaggerate rather than correct converging verticals. More serious practitioners stick with large format, describing the comparatively limited movements of smaller formats as 'feeble'.

◀ For this magnificent interior at Longleat, PETER LOWRY used rising front on a 5x4 camera with a 90mm lens, to include as much as possible of the ornate ceiling. Main lighting comes from windows to the right of the picture with a little help from 2000 Joules of umbrella flash to the left of the camera position. Notice how the tungsten table lamps and wall lights are left on to add warmth to the picture.

The other big change is that if we take architectural to mean any photography to do with buildings, then these days there seems to be a lot more work undertaken inside rather than out. With comparatively few new buildings being put up and architects all on very tight budgets, the scope for traditional architectural photography is limited, though magazines remain a source of commissions. However, the scope for interior work is much more promising. Refurbishment of existing buildings is a big business, with potential photographic work coming from interior design companies and suppliers of materials such as floor coverings, light fittings, furnishings and so on. Another useful source of commissions is annual reports – from companies proud of their offices and buildings.

Equipment Even if you decide to use a rollfilm camera or 35mm, availability of movements is essential if you want to be taken seriously. The flexibility of large format is preferable because a rising front to avoid converging verticals on tall buildings is not the only movement you'll need. For example, whether you're shooting

▶ Iᴀɴ McKɪɴɴᴇʟʟ went to Helsinki in Finland for a week to get this shot of the Heureka Science Museum. Knowing that only direct sunlight would bring out the colour and drama of the building, he returned to the same spot day after day, only to find the sky overcast. Finally, he was rewarded with five minutes of sunshine and remembers having to work incredibly fast! His persistence paid off when *The Observer Magazine* used the picture over a spread.

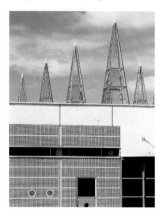

▲ Waste disposal Unit, Helsinki, by Iᴀɴ McKɪɴɴᴇʟʟ, from the same assignment.

From the space-age Science Centre near Helsinki airport (left) to the most mundane waste-disposal site (below), architecture in Finland is full of imagination, right for its purpose and reflects the spirit of the country. This is largely, says Stephen Gardiner, the result of a policy of public competition. Photographs by Ian McKinnell

BUILT TO ORDER

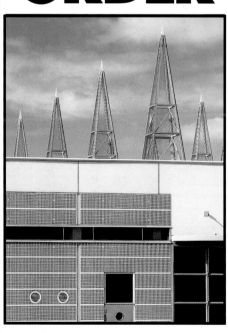

► NORMAN CHILDS took this shot of the boardroom at BP Chemicals for the company that installed the lighting. Shots of lighting istallations can be tricky because they often need to be supplemented by additional light used in a sympathetic way to enhance – rather than swamp – the existing lighting.

Diffuser light

Low-power unit bounced off wall

Diffuser light   Camera

Boardroom – BP Chemicals

inside or out, you'll sometimes find that the best viewpoint is obscured by an unwanted object such as a bollard or pillar; using 'cross front' (shifting the lens right or left of centre) the camera can be moved to the side of the obstacle, and still achieve the same viewpoint. Obviously, a sturdy tripod will also be needed and a good light meter, since long exposures are often needed.

For interior work you'll also need a lot of light. Generally flash is preferred, and for large areas up to 20,000 Joules may be required. For larger jobs, extra flash units can be hired, or existing power increased using multi-flashing.

Exteriors When shooting exteriors, the prime consideration is light. On a dull, overcast day, dramatic pictures showing the form, texture and detail of a building are impossible to obtain. Experienced clients will understand this, but on some occasions it may be necessary to warn clients just how weather-dependent good architectural photography is. If you want sharp, well defined pictures, then direct sunlight is well worth waiting for.

When faced with bad weather, one possible

◄ The weather was 'miserable' when IAN MCKINNELL took this shot of Vogans Mill in London's Docklands, for *The Observer Magazine.* A rainy, overcast day made photography virtually impossible, so MacKinnell waited till just after dusk, sheltering in a shop entrance. He needed to show the context of the building, so with available light low, he took a five-minute exposure and used 'extreme' movements to get the verticals correct.

▶ Areas as large as this hall at the worshipful Company of Drapers, need a lot of light to maintain even exposure. On this occasion NORMAN CHILDS was working for the floor covering contractor, but the client wanted a sense of the ornateness of the whole room, not just the flooring.

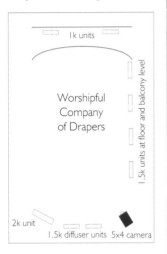

fallback solution is to take evening or night pictures, since these are not so dependent on the weather. If the building is floodlit, obviously this will help and generally interior lights should be left on. Sometimes the best moment to achieve a dramatic sky effect, purple rather than black, is just before dusk, when there is still a little light left in the sky. With experience (usually learnt by trial and error) it's possible to achieve very effective night shots of buildings and these will often be preferable to daylight pictures made in dull conditions.

Interiors Again the prime requirement is light – but most of the time you'll need to bring your own! Existing lighting may also be used, but two factors need to be watched: the colour of the light (which may range from green to orange) and the fall-off or unevenness (often not obviously apparent to the eye, but registering on film with dark shadow areas). Whenever possible, some photographers prefer to switch off all existing lights, preferring the control and consistent colour balance of flash. Sometimes, of course, the existing lighting may be an important feature of the room, in which case flash may be needed to supplement and strengthen it. This may lead to the problem of 'mixed lighting' (tungsten and flash, fluorescent and flash or even all three!).

In the old days, specialists had their own methods of dealing with mixed lighting. Since filtration was the answer to correcting colour casts which didn't match the overall film bal-

◄ Proving that architectural photographers can use smaller formats successfully, JULIAN NIEMAN took this study of Stedcombe House, Dorset, on 35mm. It was used on the cover of *Country Life* magazine. Note how the planes of the grass and the wall add interest to a very formal building – there's plenty of room for cover mentions too.

ance (either daylight or tungsten), it was not unknown for specific lights and small areas to be 'dodged in' during the exposure with a small piece of filter material attached to a wire. Today there's less call for that kind of rigour. Firstly, tastes are slightly more relaxed so that, provided they are kept to a minimum, slight colour casts from deviant lights in a picture are more readily accepted by viewers. Secondly, modern film emulsions are tend to be far more forgiving when exposed to mixed light sources, evening out colour casts in a quite satisfactory manner. Indeed, controlled use of existing lights, even when they don't match the film balance, can add a certain warmth and 'ambience' to a picture.

'Architectural work is mostly about the weather – that's the only way to get emotion and feeling into a shot. The light is everything.'

Ian McKinnell, architectural photographer

People

Everyone likes to see pictures of people – we are endlessly fascinated by our own image. And it is this very fascination that makes people such a powerful element in commercial photography. But we need to tread carefully. Photographed well, people can add life and authenticity to a picture, photographed badly, they can destroy it.

Photograph: Maske, by Sanders Nicolson

*Photographic
portraiture may
have begun as an
alternative to
painting, but very
soon the two
disciplines went
their separate ways
in terms of the
end result*

What comes naturally

E ver since our ancestors persuaded their subjects to sit still enough, pictures of people have been an essential part of photography. In those early days, of course, people pictures were very much in the tradition of portrait painting. In fact Victorian portrait photographers even adopted the language of painting, referring to themselves as 'artists' who would 'make a likeness' in the 'studio'. The tradition has been so powerful that it still exists in many photographic portrait businesses today, with large, canvass-bonded, gilt framed, colour portraits on offer, often lit and composed in the style of old masters such as Rembrandt.

Parallel with this tradition, as equipment became more portable and film emulsions faster, some photographers discovered that photography could do things that painting couldn't. Because it derived from physically recording – rather than interpreting – the light and shade of an image, photography felt closer to reality. And faster shutter speeds meant that fleeting expressions and passing gestures, could more easily be captured. Indeed, the influence now works the other way, with many

▶ **For this fashion shot,** SANDERS NICOLSON **used 'cross processing' – slide film processed in colour negative chemistry, which gives this strange blue cast to the picture. Despite the relaxed expression and informality, notice how elegantly the hand has been posed.**

painters working from photographs, or trying to recreate that mysterious 'alive' quality that a good photograph possesses.

In commercial photography, people as subjects play such an important part that it would be difficult to get through a career without having to photograph them at some time, in some shape or form. Even when they are not the principal subject, people have a habit of getting into the picture. In industrial and architectural photography, they provide a sense of scale and a reminder of human involvement. Product photographers need people to show how the products are used. Even the purest still life and food photographers may sometimes need a pouring hand or a model in the background.

There are also large areas of photography in which people are primary even though they are not the actual product being sold. Examples are 'lifestyle' pictures in advertising, most public relations photography and, of course, fashion and beauty. Even with portrait work for magazines or company reports, the real product is the story, the company or the magazine itself, not the person in the picture.

Handled properly, the human element adds vitality to a picture. But there's also a danger that perfectly acceptable compositions can be spoiled by the inclusion of human subjects posed awkwardly with wooden expressions. So, whether you specialise in shooting people or need these skills only occasionally, it's important to understand the techniques involved. Let's look at how the experts – portrait and fashion photographers, for example – approach their subject.

Preparation Obviously, being well prepared is a good idea in all branches of photography, but for shooting people, it's doubly important. That's because you need all your time and energy to be focused on coaxing the right per-

▲ **Annie Lennox by Sanders Nicolson** – again, with 'cross processing'. 'Annie has such a strong face, that I was able to light her with just a single spot and a small reflector,' he remembers.

▲ **With a little thought,** MICHAEL HEMSLEY **has transformed a fairly ordinary group shot into something special. He took the idea from the fact that this is a staff picture for a small laboratory which does colour and black and white printing. Here's how it was done:**

1 Original picture taken on colour transparency.

2 B&W negative contact printed from colour transparency.

3 B&W transparency contact printed from B&W negative.

4 On a rostrum set up over a light source, the left hand half of the B&W transparency is exposed onto colour negative duplicating film, with the right-hand side shaded with a card.

5 In the same manner, the right-hand side of the colour transparency is exposed while shading the left hand side.

formance out of your human subjects – rather than worrying about technical problems with the lighting, exposure, backgrounds and so on. This is one reason why fashion photographers, for example, generally work with an assistant, who takes care of the technical hassles.

Since human beings are easily bored and their time is usually limited (or expensive), for studio work it will pay you to set up as much as you can before they arrive. Get your lighting sorted out (it's often best to keep it simple), work out your exposures, your backgrounds and how the pictures will be framed. Equally, when away from the studio, it's best to scout out locations and angles before you start to involve your subjects. Even when allowed only five or 10 minutes to photograph a celebrity or VIP in a hotel room or office, the diligent photographer will have checked out beforehand the location and what facilities are available, often setting up lights and testing exposures before the subject arrives.

Expression All this preparation has been to one end: to allow you to concentrate on getting your subject in the right frame of mind to perform naturally in front of the camera. We could show you 10 or 20 classic lighting set-ups for portraiture – indeed whole books have been written of this topic – but they would be useless if your subject still looked wooden and lifeless. When shooting people, expression is everything. Your clients, or the public at large, might not be experts on lighting or composition, but they can certainly tell whether or not

'I prefer black and white for people. Colour doesn't add very much and can be distracting. Sometimes they turn up in terrible clothes!'

Martin Beckett

the person in the picture looks convincingly 'natural'. When it comes to expression, everyone is an expert.

The problem is that most people hate being photographed. Plonk them in front of a big camera with lots of lights around them and they freeze. Tell them to smile and things get even worse! Yet these same people probably look perfectly relaxed in a candid snap taken at a party. For the professional, the trick is to improve the technical conditions – lighting, exposure, composition, background etc – while keeping that same, relaxed, unintimidating, party atmosphere.

Mostly this is done by talking. Top portrait photographers, for example, develop an easy style of conversation – finding common ground, encouraging response, slipping in the occasional joke, keeping up a constant stream of patter no matter what the subject, so that the sitter begins to relax and forget about the ordeal of being photographed. Once the fear has gone, it becomes much easier to direct the sitter and to suggest ideas that will elicit the expression you want. These can be quite corny: for example, 'Think about what you would like to be doing most in the world...' but if they get the result, who cares? You'll probably develop your own approach – the important thing is to find out what works. Child photographers, for instance, are never afraid of making complete fools of themselves – and the children love it.

This approach may seem rather elaborate

for pictures in which people are not the main subject. But as long as you can see their faces, you still need expression. So you still need to talk, only this time you're directing a scene rather than a close-up. This can be difficult because although the activity may be familiar – operating a word processor or having a sales meeting, for example – the presence of the camera makes the situation artificial: you are asking your subjects to become actors. Once you've worked out how the picture should look, your best hope is to get your subjects so relaxed that they forget about the camera and start being natural again.

Posing Expression is vital but body language matters too. Sometimes if you can get your subject relaxed then everything else 'falls into place' and they pose naturally too. On other occasions they need a little help, especially with the way they stand. Wedding photographers usually ask the bride to angle her body by placing one foot slightly forward and placing the weight on the back hip. This might sound artificial, but from the camera angle it looks far more graceful than both feet together. Professional models will tend to adopt such poses naturally – they know what works.

Hands usually need attention too. Because they are such an important and familiar part of the body, hands can be very expressive. But from certain angles, they can look like lumps of meat. In real life, with continuous vision, we don't notice this, but the camera records one viewpoint only, so we need to make sure that it's the right one. If they are not engaged in an activity, such as holding something, then it's best to make hands as unobtrusive as possible, placing them sideways to the camera.

Finally, for commercial shots, if you want your human subjects to look good, then the wisest course is to hire good models. The best models are well paid not just because they are pretty or handsome, but because they photograph well in any situation. As any fashion photographer will tell you, the fact that models respond well to direction and can quickly run through a variety of poses and expressions, saves time and ensures a much higher percentage of usable pictures.

Shooting people

So the subject is people, but it's more complicated than that... There's a world of difference between photographing professional models and the md of the local engineering company...

In the previous section we looked at the general principles of photographing people, now it's time to get more specific. After all, there's a big difference between photographing the chairman in his office and shooting a group of models on location. So let's consider some of the situations you are likely to encounter.

Portraiture Being able to take a good portrait can be a major asset in practically any area of commercial photography. It's the kind of job that clients will expect you to be able to turn a hand to, even if your speciality doesn't normally involve people.

For the technical side, the basic rule is: keep it simple. If you decide to specialise in portrait work, then of course, you may want to experiment with elaborate lighting set-ups to give your pictures greater individuality. But for basic 'bespoke' portraiture, you shouldn't need more than a couple of umbrella flash heads and a reflector. In fact, excellent results can be obtained using just windowlight and reflectors, but since we're going for reliability and consistency, you should take the flash along

too for security. For interior work, don't be afraid to use available tungsten lighting as well – table lamps for example – though it's best to switch off any fluorescent lighting. These days mixing tungsten and daylight is perfectly acceptable, though it's preferable to keep the tungsten in the background, off the main subject.

The aim, as we discussed in the previous section, is to keep technicalities to a minimum. Having one's portrait done is enough of an ordeal without the photographer constantly mucking around with lights and testing exposures. By keeping it simple, you can concentrate on getting your sitter into the right frame of mind to give you the expressions you want. You'll also have the space to look for interesting shapes and making sure that your sitter is comfortably posed with hands looking natural, hair neat, clothes tidy and so on.

Having achieved a pleasant likeness, we may now look a little further and ask, what is the purpose of the portrait? If it was simply to flatter the sitter, then we've probably done enough. But even when a degree of flattery is tactful – in a portrait of the chairman for exam-

◄ SANDERS NICOLSON took this fashion shot for Barbour on 35mm format with a long lens as the model walked slowly up the road towards the camera. To achieve this degree of naturalness, while also showing off the clothing, usually means painstaking rehearsals and lots of takes.

ple – that may not be the primary purpose of the job. If the chairman's picture is for an annual report, then the real purpose is probably to convey a sense certain qualities associated with his position: strength, reliability, trustworthiness and so on. We may also want to identify the man with his business: if he's in the construction industry, for example, should we show him as a man of action, out on site wear-ing a hard hat as well as his normal suit and tie uniform? Given the right treatment, every picture can tell a story, so there's no reason why annual report portraits should be merely mug shots.

When we move on to editorial portraiture, the plot thickens. Instead of being an option, the story now becomes of primary importance. If the portrait of the chairman has been com-

▲ When MARTIN BECKETT turned up to photograph to photograph Rick Moranis for *Video Week*, the young comedy actor seemed very nervous. 'You need to talk at them the whole time to stop them thinking too much,' Beckett advises, 'engage them eye to eye and wait till they break off eye contact, then shoot it quick.' From the session came this unusually pensive insight from behind the professional 'mask'.

▲ 'The more famous the subject, the less time the photographer gets to take the picture. With Kirk Douglas, I got about two-and-a-half minutes,' recalls MARTIN BECKETT. 'You need instant communication and a lot of self-confidence about technique.' The theme, for *Women's Journal*, was 'Forever Spartacus', so Beckett knew he needed a heroic look. He achieved this by shooting from a low angle while his assistant held up a single strobe head.

missioned by a business magazine to go with a profile interview, then they're looking for a picture which will complement and hopefully add to the story. And since the chairman isn't paying for the picture with consequent rights of approval, there's scope for a much more imaginative treatment. In some respects, magazine work is close to advertising: the role of the picture is to sell the story.

Photographing groups Group portraits are worth a separate mention because of the special difficulties they present. There are two major considerations. Firstly, whether we are talking about three or four people or a group of 20 or 30, we need to see the shape of the group

as an entity in itself. In other words, to avoid the whole thing looking like a school photo, we need to distribute the elements of the group in a way that produces an interesting but coherent shape. We should also bear in mind that the focus of interest is always the face, so we need to try and spread these interest points around the frame rather than having them in a straight line. In simple situations, this is achieved by mixing people of different heights and having some people standing and others sitting. Another solution is to take a high viewpoint and have your group look up to the camera: this enables you to create a shape made entirely of faces.

Once we've got the group well shaped, we can concentrate on the second consideration which is that any group shot is also a series of individual portraits. It's therefore important to engage the attention of everyone present, since it only takes one person spoil the picture. Blinking is another problem: with a large group it's virtually impossible to watch everyone at once – your only possible insurance is to shoot at least a couple of rolls of film.

Working with models Models are people whose job depends on being photographed. Unlike other people you may have to shoot, this gives them a greater stake in the end product: they want to help you achieve good pictures, because that what they're paid for and good pictures may lead to more work. But unfortunately, good looks and a willingness to help, doesn't always guarantee that the pictures will work. That's why specialists in advertising and fashion often have favourite models that they use again and again. Just as they may have a favourite camera or film, these photographers know that there are certain models with whom they have a good working relationship, and who can be relied upon to deliver the goods.

The secret is good casting. When a new model walks into the studio, even the most experienced fashion photographers cannot know for certain how he or she will photograph. If you've got an important job coming up, the only way to find out for sure is to shoot a test, or try out the model first on something less important. In the long run, the extra time it takes to make sure the casting is right, will always pay dividends. If the model is wrong or looks lifeless, you can bet your client will spot it straight away,

whether or not he's a good judge of photography in general.

Children Some photographers are wary about working with children and it's true to say that they need a slightly different approach to adult subjects. One difference is that providing you create the right conditions, whether or not they are being paid as models, most children – up to the age of about 12 – actually enjoy being photographed. By encouraging a free-and-easy atmosphere, you can use this natural enthusiasm to your advantage, though of course, there

'Fashion photography illustrates a mood, a feeling, it creates a fantasy to capture the imagination, to inspire the public to buy certain clothes so that they can become part of that fantasy. We sell the illusion of a perfect look to people who are less than perfect.'

Zanna Wilford, fashion photographer

◄ For this picture of Placido Domingo for a record cover, MARTIN BECKETT had to think on his feet. The brief called for the great singer to be photographed in front of this ornate old theatre in Madrid. However, at street level, the theatre was littered with concrete mixers, so Beckett popped over the road and talked the owner of the apartment opposite to let him photograph from her balcony. That gave him the right viewpoint for the singer to sit in the first floor window of the theatre, with the ornate mouldings nicely filling the square format of the record cover. Another job in the bag.

also needs to be an underlying element of discipline if you want to get the job finished!

The best thing about young children is their naturalness and spontaneity. Once you have visualised the picture, positioned them, and told them what the story is, there's little need for posing or direction, you just let them get on with it. With practice, you can even coax a performance out of babies and toddlers – according to the experts, it's just a matter of getting onto their wavelength. Then, providing you've prepared the technical side – simple wrap-around lighting is best – you should get good pictures.

PR photography Although the PR market also covers product photography, what we want to consider here is pictures of people and events. Indeed, this type of photography is the staple diet of small agencies throughout the country.

▲ In situ portrait of Sir Gil Thompson, chief executive of Manchester Airport, by IAN COATES. For executive portraiture, Coates believes that preparation is essential. In this case he visited the airport the day before to check out the VIP lounge and make sure that the aircraft would be in view. He used fill-in flash and a long exposure to get the background through the tinted glass. 'On location,' says Coates, 'simplicity is the key – you don't have time to mess around.'

Their mission is to get their clients into print – national newspapers and consumer magazines would be nice, but more realistically, local press and specialist business magazines.

The usual technique is to create a story out of an event, such as the opening of a factory or office, or perhaps an 'open day' or anniversary celebration. Where possible a celebrity may be involved to help make the story more attractive. Here, photography can play an important role, especially where local papers are concerned. What is required is an all-in-one news shot – usually set up – which looks lively on the page and also manages to 'sell' the company or product the agency wants to feature.

Unfortunately, it has to be said that the general standard of such PR photography in this country is rather uneven. Typical mistakes include presentation or 'shaking hands' pictures (a boring idea anyway) with far too much space between the presenter and the recipient. News pictures need to be kept tight so that they can be cropped in and still get the message across. Photographers in this field would do well to study the work of their colleagues in the press world – indeed some of the best PR shots are done by ex-newspaper photographers.

▲ This studio portrait by IAN COATES shows the importance of expression and naturally posed hands. Designed for press use, the picture is composed so that it can be used either as is, or cropped for a tighter head-and-shoulders image. 'Expression is what sells a portrait,' he says, 'many photographers press the shutter too late.'

◄ PR photography is about personalities, but it's also about exposure for the companies that pay the bill. In this example by BILL PRUDOM, the main attraction is Les Dawson, but the two sponsors, Raleigh Bicycles and the Copthorne Hotel are also included. Notice also how Prudom has kept the composition tight – the preferred style for local newspapers who like to see pictures bursting out of the page.

◄ In this PR shot for Britannia Airways, BILL PRUDOM livens up a standard long-service employee shot, by including two air hostesses and an aircraft. Notice again, how tight he keeps the composition – it could be cropped in without losing the message.

Advertising

Sometimes you sell the sizzle,
sometimes you sell the steak.
Advertising photography can be about
creating moods or simply shifting
boxes. Either way there tends to be a
lot of money involved and for the
photographer who can handle the
stress and deliver the quality, rewards

• Very much a soft-sell 'sizzle' picture, this
Scottish landscape by SANDERS NICOLSON for
Barbour, sells the lifestyle rather than the actual
product. Shot at dusk, in rainy conditions, it took
an hour-and-a-half to cope with the constantly
changing light and to position the boatman via

that Pictures pay

Advertising work can be the most lucrative for the photographer. Is there a good reason why the 'glamour' end of the business should pay so well?

Without doubt, advertising photography is the 'glamour' end of the profession. Fees tend to be far higher than for straight 'commercial' photography (for brochures, sales leaflets and so on) and with sustained success comes the chance of real prosperity.

Why should this be so? How can one photographer, taking product pictures for a local company earn, say £250, while another photographer taking similar product shots for a London advertising agency, is paid ten times that amount? Even after paying London rents and rates for his studio, the advertising specialist makes far more money for what, to the layman, might appear to be much the same job.

The basic difference is the arena of work. Advertising is a big money business. When the agency and its team – market researchers, media specialists, writers, designers, typographers, photographers and so on – gets an advertising campaign right, the client company stands to increase sales by millions of pounds. Even if the campaign doesn't work, it still costs huge amounts of money because production fees and media space costs (newspapers, magazines, colour supplements and so on) are so high. So an agency – which is judged only by results – is prepared to pay large amounts of money to hire the people it thinks will ensure that the campaign succeeds. And this is why a handful of photographers, with proven track records, seem to get all the best jobs.

In some respects, advertising photography is a bit like acting. An actor may be doing perfectly good work in repertory or fringe theatre, then suddenly comes the big break: West End theatre, television or films. Suddenly his or her income moves into an entirely different bracket. What has changed is not the ability of the actor but the arena of work. In practice, the performance of the actor may improve, due to contact with more talented actors and directors, but the basic talent remains constant.

The casualty rate is similar too. It's well known that for every actor who succeeds, probably a thousand are having a hard time with little or no work. Perhaps the competition in advertising photography isn't quite so harsh, but with thousands of 'qualified' students joining the market every year, even man-

aging to earn a modest living can be an uphill battle.

So what are the ingredients of success? Faced with this kind of competition, most photographers agree that the primary requirement is commitment. Even to get a job as an assistant, may require hundreds of letters, telephone calls and interviews. This requires boundless energy and an unflagging spirit, but the more people you see, the more you learn about the business. In a similar manner, fledgling actors are advised to attend as many auditions as possible, however demoralising rejections may seem at the time.

In fact, getting to see a photo buyer, such as an agency art director, is not difficult. The industry thrives on new talent and new ideas, so nobody wants to pass up the possibility of a new discovery. But though buyers may be willing to see new talent, it's a far bigger step to actually hire an untried photographer for a job. The buyer needs to feel confident that the photographer can deliver.

What are the factors most likely to influence buyers? Personal qualities like commitment and enthusiasm are important, but the work in the portfolio must stand up too. Here we get back to that special feeling which we described in Chapter 2 'Basics' as 'quality'. To simplify matters, we broke down this down into technical and creative quality – even though in the best pictures, it's difficult to separate the two.

In some respects, technical quality is the most important, because without it, you won't even get started. In the advertising business – more than any other sector of the profession – high technical standards are assumed to be the norm. This is because art directors are so used to working with good photographers, that they quickly become attuned to high standards, so

that anything less than 'professional quality' immediately becomes glaringly obvious.

It's also worth remembering that, contrary to the popular image, the majority of advertising assignments are 'bread and butter' work and do not call for great creative artistry. The photographer is simply required to translate the visual idea of the designer or art director into a competent photograph. What is expected is not creative flair, but superb technical quality.

Having said that, without a degree of creative individuality or 'personal style', it's difficult to get noticed. Although most photographers are uncomfortable with the idea of

being 'pigeon-holed', in a competitive field it's inevitable that specialists get remembered for a particular type of work. To the buyer, a belief in specialists helps reduce apparent risks. Hiring any photographer for a job is a gamble – no one knows for sure how the pictures will turn out – so let's improve the odds by hiring someone with a known track record in the type of photography we need.

But we wouldn't want to give the impression that all art directors play safe. The best creative people are always adventurous and will naturally be drawn to photographers with a similar urge to develop new ways of seeing and representation. This is why the best advertising photographers usually spend a lot of time on personal work and 'testing'. Like their clients, they are visually sophisticated people, always looking for fresh angles and new techniques to surprise and delight their viewers.

• Advertising photographer PETER DAZELEY was proud of how close he managed to get this finished result to the rough visual of art director Rick Wright (SMI Advertising). Since Dazeley's studio had neither sufficient height nor stage lighting, the key requirement was to find the right location. After a day spent scouting through London theatres and clubs, taking reference pictures and matching hire charges to the budget, a club in Brixton was finally chosen. The shot was lit with tungsten stage lighting. Once the speakers had been stacked up, they were placed on the stage and shot from below with a wideangle lens to match the perspective of the visual. Dazeley notes with wry amusement that one photographer had apparently included in his quote for this job, the cost of model making the speakers in distorted perspective!

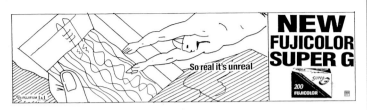

▲ When CARL LYTTLE was asked to shoot a 96-sheet poster advertisement for Fujicolor Super G, this pencil sketch from art director Simon Thompson (Mike Sigrist Associates) was the only guidance he received. The ad had to keep in theme with the TV commercial slogan 'So real it's unreal', but there was no colour direction. What's more, pressure was intense because poster sites had already been booked. The job took only one week, including location shots in Miami, studio work and image manipulation. Lyttle's memory of the shoot: Panic!

• A realistic swimming pool for the 'print' seemed essential, so Lyttle flew to Miami the day after receiving the brief. There he went round hotel swimming pools with a ladder, photographing ripple effects. In the event, the water from one pool was combined electronically with the edge of another.
NB Please overprint the crop marks on these two trannies, though it might be clearer if they printed, say, yellow rather than black as on originals.

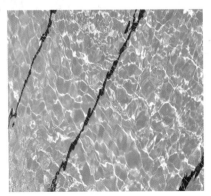

▲ The final composite after manipulation on the Crosfield Mamba system: the sky colour has been enhanced, perspective altered on the pool and false shadows added to connect the 'print' with the diver.

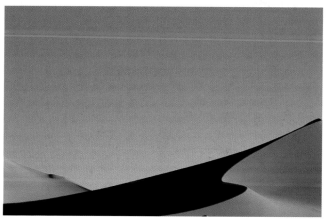

▲ The sand dune was a stock shot from Images Colour Library – with a fairly standard element like this, it's a lot cheaper to buy from stock than to fly out to the nearest desert!

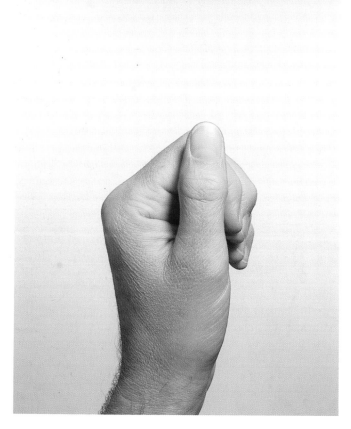

• The diver and hand model were shot in the studio. Since he was to be cropped, the diver could be shot standing, with plenty of side lighting to simulate overhead sunshine.

Sharing the risk

In advertising there are a number of people who can become involved in producing the end product – art directors, stylists, models…

▲ **This 'lifestyle' picture for Raleigh bicycles by SANDERS NICOLSON, is a good example of teamwork. It was shot in Provence in the early morning, just after sunrise – not just any sunrise either, it took three mornings to get the light right. To create the 'mist' effect, Nicolson had his assistants and other crew members light fires with damp leaves and flap the smoke through the trees. Finally the models themselves played an important part: Nicolson uses them a lot because 'they work incredibly well together as a couple.' 'When all the elements come together,' he says, 'you get the right picture.'**

While it may be romantic to see the advertising photographer as a creative artist – or image manager – who creates wonderful images from scratch, the reality is usually different. As we mentioned earlier, advertising is a big money business and most of the 'money people' have neither the patience nor the resources to allow photographers complete freedom. In a few isolated cases, that sort of freedom may be given, but generally the photographer works as part of a creative team.

Depending on the campaign, a good deal of work may have been done before the photographer is even commissioned. In product advertising, for example, detailed research will have been carried out into the buying habits, preferences and perceptions of the likely buyers. A target market will have been established, together with a feeling of how the product or range of products will slot into that market. Creative ideas will have been developed in rough and probably tested on selected consumers. The recommended idea will then be 'sold' to the client backed up by details of research findings. After much discussion and

probably, some modification, the client will agree that the advertisement should go on to its next phase – the actual production.

This explains why photographers are often presented with quite tight layout visuals with apparently little room to manoeuvre. The client is spending large amounts of his company's money on the advertisement and is therefore nervous of any deviation from the agreed formula. He tends to be backed up by the agency's 'account handler' or 'account executive' whose job it is to look after the client. What they sometimes seem to forget is that there is no magic formula, all advertising involves risk and just because something has been agreed does not guarantee that it will succeed. The result of keeping too a tight rein on the creative team, is usually 'safe' boring advertising.

What can the photographer contribute? In this type of situation, the best he or she can do is to translate the visual into an image of superb technical quality. In fact, this may help a great deal. The reason why photography is used so much in advertising is that its visual appeal is second to none. If the photography is good enough, it can lift a fairly mundane idea, creating something eye-catching and even memorable. Good art directors realise this, which is why they are always happy to see talented new photographers.

At the basic level then, the job of the photographer is to translate the visual ideas of the art director into photographic terms. Sometimes the technical challenges involved even in straight translation of a visual idea, may be formidable. With the advent of digital imaging and manipulation, for example, the boundaries of imagination become extended. An art director who knows the capabilities of the photographer, may give free rein to all sorts of surrealistic compositions. In such cases, creating pictures as close as possible to the original sketch, will be a considerable achievement.

On most jobs, as we have indicated, the photographer is part of a creative team. Ideally, this means literally that everyone has a contribution to make so that the sum of the achievement becomes greater than its parts. We already have a fair idea about the role of the photographer, let's take a look at the other major players.

The art director/client A very important person, not least because he or she pays the bill! Depending on the job, a representative of the client company may or may not be present at the shoot. If such a representative does come along, some photographers prefer to exclude them tactfully from the studio itself – this is where a comfortable reception area and plenty of good coffee proves invaluable. In any case, for creative purposes, the photographer's real client is the art director – it's very difficult to work creatively for more than one person simultaneously.

As in any profession, art directors come in all shapes and sizes – good, bad and indifferent. As we've already suggested, an indifferent art director with mediocre ideas, should not preclude the photographer from doing a good job. However, a good art director will certainly make producing good work a lot easier. He or she will understand the technical and creative contribution that the photographer can make and, as far as possible, will allow enough freedom for that contribution to be made. At the same time, the good art director will also push, encourage and inspire the photographer, refusing to accept easy solutions.

The photographer's assistant The basic job of the assistant is to look after the technical requirements: checking lighting and exposure, loading cameras and so on. Naturally, the photographer should also be aware of these technicalities and is quite capable of handling them alone. However, on an important job, there are many other things to think about and since a technical fault can ruin everything, the insur-

ance of having someone else looking out for errors, can be invaluable. When things get tough, it also helps to have an ally, someone 'in your corner', either to bounce ideas off, or in extreme cases, to hold you together!

The stylist Depending on the nature of the job and the size of the budget, a stylist may be used as 'another pair of eyes'. Usually the stylist brings to the shoot some kind of specialised knowledge or experience. Their basic concern is with the look and content of the picture – so they will often supply accessories or props, even the location. Sometimes their contribution can be vital to the success of the picture. In fashion work, for example, the stylist is involved with the fashion 'look' – what goes together and how the clothes themselves come across. Sometimes they may also take responsibility for make-up and hairstyling, though these key jobs are often handled by specialists. In a similar way, a food stylist looks after the style of the food in a picture, often preparing and arranging it.

The model For shots involving people, it's usual to use models. This is not just to cover the question of copyright, but also because, as any fashion photographer will tell you, good models can make a major difference to the success of a picture. Basically they know what works in pictures – whether it's a pose, an expression or acting out a 'lifestyle' situation. This is why the best models are well paid. With less experienced (and cheaper) models, you could get the result you were after, but it would take a lot more film and a lot more time.

Other creative contributors For certain pictures, specialists may be hired as and when they are needed. Into this category come such people as set designers and constructors, and model makers. Since much of this work is highly specialised, you'll probably get the job done better by using an expert.

Finishers Not actually involved in the shoot, but very much involved with the image making process, are finishers such as colour and monochrome printers. Specialist black and white printers have always had a following, but now that colour prints are becoming more acceptable where once only transparencies were permitted, colour printers are also making an important contribution. As we show in Chapter 12 (Processing), a good printer can make a dramatic difference to the final appearance of an image. By the same token, we should also mention that photographic printers have their counterparts in digital imaging, whether at bureaux or repro houses. In advertising, the process is not really finished until the image has appeared in print.

Personal work

There's far more to personal work than mere self-indulgence. For one thing, it's a way of developing an individual style and building up an impressive portfolio

For the photographer who makes a career in commercial work, the constant demand for fresh ideas and technical perfectionism, can be draining. To maintain his or her reputation, a photographer may be expected to perform at the top level, constantly supplying new creative solutions to familiar problems, over a period of thirty years or more. The danger, of course, is that work becomes repetitive and the solutions start to conform to a formula – the photographer gets into a rut.

This is why many photographers find it important to 'get back to their roots', taking pictures for themselves in an effort to recapture the joy in creativity and experimentation that first attracted them to photography. This is particularly true in the advertising field where competitive demands are at their most severe, but it is equally necessary for other types of commercial photography. Discoveries made and confidence gained in personal work – often called 'testing' – regularly feeds through into commercial work, revitalising it and giving fresh impetus.

Personal work can also be a way of freeing the photographer from the daily constraints of working in restricted styles to tight briefs. Often specialist photographers will choose a completely different field for personal work: so we find food photographers doing nudes, or fashion photographers involved in still life pictures. Personal work becomes a refuge, an escape from the daily grind. So in some ways it's ironic that it may also become an important way of attracting the attention of clients.

Art directors, designers and other visually sophisticated buyers, are interested in personal work for two reasons. Firstly it offers the potential of a ready-made idea which may fit their particular needs. By its very nature, personal work has not been used commercially before, so the buyer can conveniently adapt the particular 'look' the photographer has achieved. The second reason applies only to buyers with rather more confidence in their own judgment. When developed seriously, personal work gives a much better indication of a photographer's potential ability, than does commercial work. So the art director who wants to create something original, rather than copying existing styles, will always look for the

◀ Some photographers have such an individual style that practically all their work could be called 'personal'. Just look at the graphic simplicity of this strawberry in clotted cream by TESSA TRAEGER. She developed her pictorial style over many years of food illustration for Vogue, enjoying the kind of personal freedom to experiment and interpret her subjects, that the more prosaic world of advertising photography, might not have allowed.

evidence of natural talent and flair which tends to come through more clearly in personal work.

Basically, personal work gives the photographer the chance to do things that he or she may not have been given the opportunity to do in commercial practice. In an effort to push the language of photography forward, new techniques can be explored and rules broken. In the printing and processing area, for example, some photographers have become fascinated by old processing techniques. It's a fascination that stems from asking questions about accepted practices: why should an evenly exposed, sharp, fine grained, colour saturated transparency, be the only way to represent reality?

'I do a lot of personal work – it's really the only reason I do the commercial work: tax-free film and cameras etc'

Chris Joyce, advertising photographer

By altering the look and feel of a photograph, perhaps with soft, pastel shades, exaggerated grain or posterised colours, we can force the viewer to look more closely at the image. Too much of anything leads to comfortable clichés. Like any language, in order to remain fresh and effective, photography needs to continually re-invent itself.

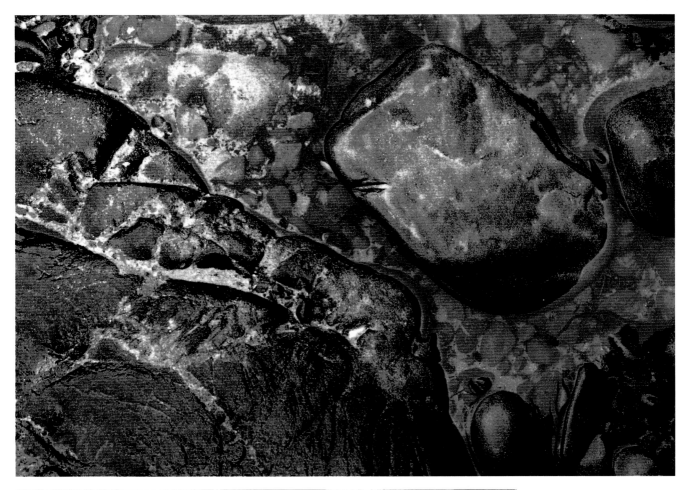

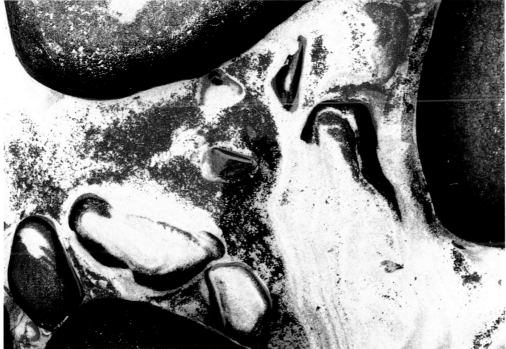

• For several years, SANDERS NICOLSON has been shooting a series on 'found objects' – natural forms, stones, rope, leaves and so on – all over the world. Eventually, he'd like to show them in an exhibition, but he'd be the first to admit that that's not really the point. In his professional life he works to briefs, always trying to portray his subjects in a way that will help sell products. With this personal series, the cardinal rule is that nothing must be touched or re-arranged. 'They are honest pictures,' he says simply.

• For CARL LYTTLE, personal work gives him the chance to experiment and explore the nature of photographic representation. His monochrome studies of mushrooms and tomatoes remind us how the presence of colour can sometimes distract from the beauty of natural forms. The subtle, soft, impressionistic colours of the leaf composition show how recreating early colour print processes can add another dimension to our idea of colour photography.

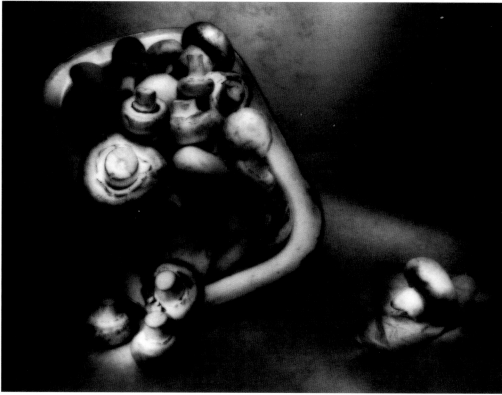

Stock

No longer an easy option for your out-takes or holiday snaps, modern stock photography demands as much dedication and professionalism as any other part of the profession. Whether you place your work with an agency or run your own library, for those with the right attitude, there's good money to be earned, particularly from 'generic', multi-purpose pictures. And the big bonus is that the right image is like money invested at a good interest rate – it just goes on earning

Taking stock

Many photographers have still to cotton onto the potential substantial earnings in stock pictures. To succeed, however, involves rather more than simply digging out your old forgotten out-takes

▶ **Landscape photographer** **TOM MACKIE makes a good living from stock photography, mainly for the calendar market. This attractive winter study of Derwentwater in the Lake District, 'sells every year' for calendars, Christmas cards and brochures. Mackie, who runs his own library, reckons that winter shots sell particularly well – they look good and not many photographers can be bothered to take them. For this shot, Mackie needed to be up and out before dawn in temperatures around -6°C. Stock calendar images like this sell for between £100 and £250 per use, and because there's nothing to date them, could go on selling for 15-20 years. First publication rights on commissioned calendars (Mackie always retains copyright) sell for £400 or £500.**

Although many never get around to it, the idea of placing work with picture libraries, appeals to most photographers. After all, all those boxes of transparencies from your holidays or out-takes from location jobs, aren't doing you much good just sitting there and gathering dust, are they? So why not sort them out and pack them off to a picture agency where they can earn you some money?

Nice idea, but according to all the libraries we have spoken to, the stock business just doesn't work like that. Nowadays libraries are mostly supplied by specialists who understand the business and know exactly what the requirements are. They may not work full-time at taking stock pictures (though some do), but they certainly don't regard the work as an afterthought or

spin-off activity. If you have the talent and the right attitude, it's possible to earn good money from stock, and once you've got the knack, the harder you work, the more you can earn.

So who is the new stock photographer?

Something of an all-rounder it would seem. He or she has the talent to spot a good picture, the discipline to ensure that requirements are met, and an absolute obsession about technical quality. Good planning is also essential and the ability to come up with unusual angles and original interpretations: sometimes the stock photographer has to act as an art director too.

Of course, if you've been in photography for some time, particularly if you work in a specialised field and your records are good, then you may consider starting your own library. But in most cases, it would probably be wiser to test the water first by submitting work to a picture agency. After all, libraries have had to learn the hard way what sells and what doesn't – if they hadn't, they wouldn't still be in business!

Choosing the right library may take time. In a recent directory, the British Association of Picture Libraries and Agencies (BAPLA), listed over 300 members, giving access, by their calculation, to over 250 million pictures. Some of these libraries are very small and very specialised, so if your interest is in general stock work, it would be best to start with the dozen or so major agencies.

Initially, most libraries require a minimum

• A series of library images from ACE PHOTO AGENCY: Champagne by AITCH, family in field by MICHAEL BLUESTONE, girl in lingerie (hand coloured) by IAN SPRATT, girl in Maldives by STEEL PHOTOGRAPHY. All these shots have that 'generic' quality that stock agencies look for: they could be used for a variety of purposes. Payment depends on the application – so you only have to strike it lucky with an advertising use for your earnings from one image to move rapidly into four figures.

submission of between 100 and 500 pictures, with 200 being typical. Commission is usually 50% of the repro fee per use. Copyright normally stays with the photographer; once-off reproduction rights are sold with the transparency being loaned out for a specific period of time. If

idea. Where possible it's also important to sort pictures into subject areas, especially where the same subject has been given several different treatments. Be ruthless in your selection of images, particularly where sharpness and exposure are concerned: the business is very competitive, so anything of doubtful technical quality won't stand a chance.

Generic appeal It stands to reason that if one picture can be used for lots of different applications, then you and your library are going to make more money from it. The word agencies use to describe this broadness of appeal is 'generic'. Think of a subject - let's take business. There are hundreds of outlets for general 'business' pictures. It might be a round table conference or perhaps new technology – computers, video conferencing and so on. A generic image is not easy to achieve: it will need an idea, plenty of impact, people who act convincingly and equipment which is not too identifiable. Pictures like this will take a lot more time and money to set up than your average travel shot, but if you get them right, they could be used tens or even hundreds of times. Other examples of generic themes are 'lifestyle' (affluent young people, cars, mobile phones, electronic equipment and so on), 'families', 'outdoor life and health' and 'teenagers'.

Individuality Again, remember that unless your area is very specialised, then you and your agency will be competing against hundreds of similar images on the same subject. So it will pay to make that extra effort to find an unusual angle or an inventive interpretation which perhaps puts the subject in a new light. Stock photography is a marketplace, pure and simple – your work will only sell if it gets noticed.

▲ Very much a 'concept picture', this image by ZEPHYR PHOTOGRAPHY for ACE PHOTO LIBRARY, brings together many themes: new technology, ease of use, education, the future and so on. Not only is the shot itself very appealing, it also lends itself to a variety of copy lines. Its only weakness – difficult to avoid – is that the equipment itself will soon look dated.

your work is accepted, however, you'll need to be patient – it can easily take up to a year for pictures to be catalogued, promoted, come to the notice of a client, ordered and finally paid for!

It's always best to contact the library first, to discuss their requirements. They may then arrange to see you or ask you to send samples of your work. Once a relationship is formed, occasionally agencies will actually commission work or at least give you a shot list of pictures they need. What are they looking for?

Quality Around 75% of agencies now accept 35mm transparencies, though often with the proviso that quality needs to be 'exceptional'. In practice, medium format slides are still more acceptable in most cases – partly because, irrespective of repro considerations, they look more impressive and are easier to view. Pictures need to be pin sharp, with as much depth of field as possible, good colour saturation and accurate exposure. In general, crisp, brightly lit, well defined, fine-grain pictures will sell better than moody, 'pastel' studies. Since we're asking these pictures to 'sell themselves', they need to be bright, eye-catching and in terms of technical quality, absolutely above reproach.

Presentation Transparencies need to be mounted, dated and captioned. Brief details of location and subject are usually all that is required, though sometimes additional information, about local customs for example, may help to sell an

'I would rather have five quality shots than 50 shots of low quality. Gone are the days when we took in pics irrespective of quality, in case they might be needed'

John Panton, Ace Photo Agency

• Reflections are big in the calendar market, says TOM MACKIE, in fact one publisher produces a successful calendar solely devoted to them. Mackie's Herringfleet Windpump, Suffolk (above) has the added advantage of showing a windmill, another popular subject. The Buttermere, Lake District, shot (left) is another study with timeless appeal. Mackie shoots mostly on 5x4: 'I like the control that the movements give and I enjoy working slowly,' he says. He reckons that large transparencies also have a psychological appeal to his clients. Calendar buyers are usually only concerned about sales of an image to their immediate competitors, sales to other markets don't bother them.

Digital

The digital imaging train is gathering speed. Should we all climb on board? Maybe we should. But how much is the ticket? And do we know the destination? Could we still get there by conventional means? Radical new technologies often throw up as many questions as answers...

▶ Digitised composite for Mercury Communications, art directed by 'The Team', from original photographs by PETER DAZELEY, who also directed the electronic comping work at Colour Unlimited.

Altered images

Image manipulation is almost as old as photography itself but never before have we heard so much fuss made about it. So just what is the appeal of electronics?

▲ A drawback of digital systems is that it's not easy to get good quality hard copies (ie colour prints) at a reasonable price. One neat solution is the Fujix Pictrography 3000, a digital image printer, which uses laser diodes to expose a donor film. This image is then transferred to a receiver material and thermally developed using wet chemistry similar to that employed by the successful Fuji Pictrostat 200 print-to-print copier. Fuji reckons an A4 colour print made on the Pictrography costs around £3.

These days a book like this would be considered incomplete without a section on digital imaging. The pressure is irresistible. Manufacturers are spending millions on research and promotion, writers are filling acres of space with lengthy explanations and arguments about this wonderful new technology. And a strange new crop of pictures is springing up all around us: weird, distorted, surrealistic.

What does it all mean? In the section to follow, we'll consider the technology itself and how it fits into the larger context. But as an introduction, let's pause for a moment and think about the creative possibilities of digital imaging and why it appeals to so many people.

Ever since the invention of photography there has always been a fascination with tricks and illusions. In fact many of the elaborate composites manipulated on today's digital 'workstations', can still be achieved (rather less expensively) with a rostrum or copy camera and soft edge masking. The reason that trick photography fascinates so many people, goes back to that old truism, 'The camera never lies'. Because a normal photograph faithfully records the likeness of an instant in time, photography has a built-in credibility that other visual media, such as painting and drawing, lack. This credibility, the idea that photography is somehow 'closer to life', is the main reason for its extensive use in advertising and commercial work. People trust a photograph.

To greater and lesser degrees, this trust places a burden of responsibility on the photographer. Which is why in photojournalism and reportage – areas where the trust factor is highest – there's such an outcry at any suggestion that pictures have been set up or manipulated. The same feeling pertains to commercial photography. Even though some people may be aware of the devices often used in food photography, for example, they want to believe that the pictures are 'real'. In fact, most such devices are intended to make the food look fresher and closer to reality.

With much of the current crop of digitally manipulated pictures, things are rather different. Faces contort in impossible distortions, tropical and arctic scenes are mixed, inherently large and small objects are transposed. There's no doubt that many of these pictures have impact, but is that enough? Is the reaction a disbelieving 'Yuk!' rather than an admiring 'Wow!'?

Part of the trouble is that many of the photographers involved don't really understand what they are doing. Like a child with a new paintbox, they suddenly have access to an almost unlimited range of possible manipulations, and they create something rather messy. The manufacturers must also accept some responsibility since many of these strange pictures are intended to promote their equipment. In this context, a weird, surrealistic image is obviously considered more eye-catching than more sober digital applications such as page make-up, product colour changes or electronic retouching.

As with 'straight' photography, it comes down to a question of meaning. Every good picture has a story or an intent behind it. There's very little point in manipulation for its own sake, or simply to create an impact by distorting accepted reality. To satisfy the viewer, a picture needs to be saying something. And this is certainly true in commercial photography, where communicating ideas about products or services is the principle aim.

This is not to say that manipulation has no role to play in commercial photography. Surrealism – the idea of combining unexpected, disparate elements into one picture – can be a very effective means of communicating ideas. But it's important to retain a link with reality – through consistent lighting, composition, perspective control and so on. The power of such pictures comes from persuading the viewer that apparently all these strange things really did come together at the same time. It's no accident that Rene Magritte – the Surrealist painter who has been a major influence on advertising imagery – painted with an almost photographic realism. If he was around today, perhaps he would have chosen digital imaging!

A prime candidate for image manipulation in the commercial area, is electronic and computer equipment. The problem, of course, is that computers are inherently boring as objects: little more than white or grey plastic boxes. Keyboards and screens don't exactly set the heart racing either! What we really want to know about computers is what they can do, how they can help us with our work. And this is not an easy idea to communicate with normal 'in camera' photography. Once we've projected screen shots onto the operator's face and exploited the graphic possibilities of microchips and printed circuit boards, is there anything left?

As we've suggested, digital imaging opens up a whole world of possibilities. But too much choice can be a dangerous thing. Left to their own devices, some photographers produce composite pictures which ignore all the rules of elegance and simplicity normally associated with their work. The best results are often obtained by good photographers working with good art directors or visualisers. Make no mistake: composite pictures are difficult to do well – not just in a technical sense but on aesthetic grounds too. It can help to have someone else visualise the picture and keep the ideas strong but simple.

Finally, another plea for credibility. In the commercial arena, some of the very best 'comped' pictures are those that the viewer believes implicitly, never suspecting that any tricks have been played.

'The future is rosy and very digital – though so far there are not enough digital clients. But in 12-18 months time it will be de rigeur to have the full system for storage and transmission.'

John Panton, Ace Photo Agency

▼ Image bureaux such as Style 10, use high-end image processing systems like this Crosfield Mamba. They are very expensive but have two major advantages over cheaper systems. Firstly they produce higher quality results and secondly they work much faster – an important consideration in the impatient world of marketing and advertising.

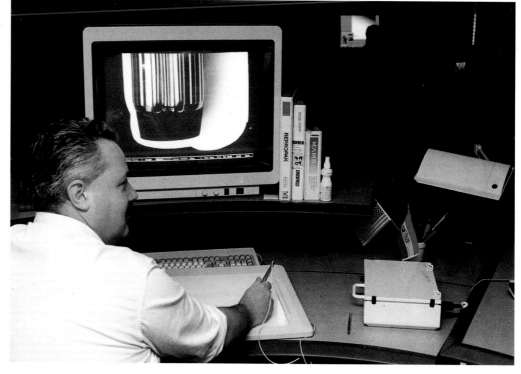

'At this time I see no point in equipping for digital imaging. I want to use the best equipment and have experts handle it for me – so I go to a bureau,' says advertising photographer PETER DAZELEY. To produce this Elonex ad for client Matthew Poppy, Dazeley took the component transparencies to Tapestry, where they were manipulated and assembled, under his direction, on a Quantel Paintbox. Piotr Henning was the art director.

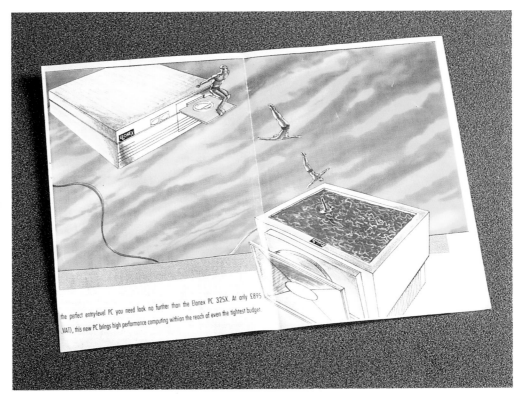

the perfect entry-level PC you need look no further than the Elonex PC 325X. At only £895 (VAT), this new PC brings high performance computing within the reach of even the tightest budget

▲ This was the original sketch layout Dazeley was given to work to.

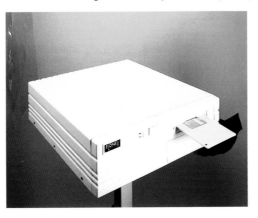

◀ The computer and monitor were fairly simple to shoot – with digital image manipulation, you don't need to worry about messy backgrounds.

▲ Carefully lit, the diver takes his starting position. Behind him can be seen the trampoline used for the next two images.

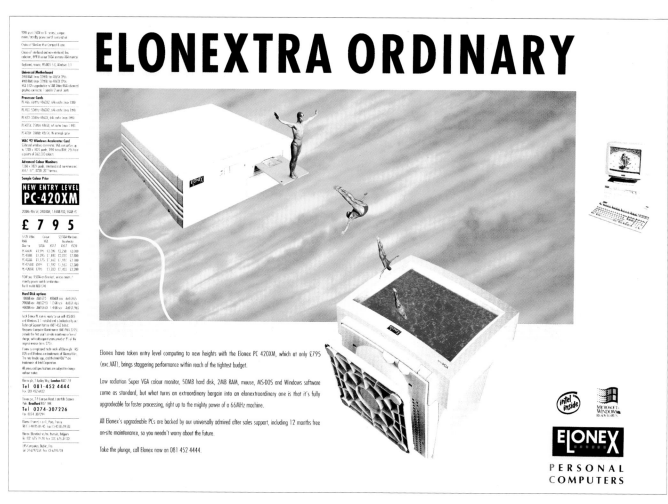

'Computers have made a tremendous difference to what's possible...'

Peter Dazeley, advertising photographer

▲ The final composite as it appeared in the finished advertisement.

▲ At first, Dazeley was uncertain how to achieve the diver's flight through the air. Then the idea of using a trampoline occurred.

▲ The diver plunges into a swimming pool. As far as possible, all four shots had to be matched for lighting and consistency of angle.

Too many photographers have seen the coming of digital photography as a threat to their livelihoods. Modern technology offers opportunities, not competition

Digital dilemmas

Since the first prototype all-electronic cameras were shown in the early 1980s, most photographers have been aware of an impending revolution in imaging. At first, the reaction from many was fear: here's a new technology which will replace everything we know and probably put us out of a job. But, as the bandwagon started rolling and more and more major manufacturers climbed on board, urging the technology in different directions, fear among photographers was replaced by confusion: we feel we should get involved, but how does all this fit into the work we do?

To get a clearer picture, we need to look at the wider context. Electronic imaging is just one part of a larger revolution in digital technology. Basically, this process involves breaking down information into simple, unchangeable, electronic components, so that it can be stored, processed, transmitted and reassembled by computers or other electronic devices; the technology is identical in principle to that behind the audio compact disk. The potential for digital technology is enormous. Already it is used extensively in business, scientific research, audio reproduction, video,

television, telecommunications, industrial design and publishing.

For example, every letter of every word you read on this page has been electronically digitised. So have instructions on the typeface and the exact position of words on the page. So have all the pictures. In fact, since roughly the time of that first all-electronic prototype camera, publishing has undergone an almost complete conversion to digital technology.

Why hasn't the same thing happened in photography? Basically because, in most respects, photography was already a highly sophisticated, convenient, cost-effective technology. Consider what it offers. For around £10, you can buy a compact, 'single-use' camera, take 24 pictures, and still have change to get them processed into perfectly acceptable colour prints. With digital technology this just isn't possible and probably won't be for many years. What's more there's still a big gap in technical quality; whereas the average 35mm transparency contains around 30 million pixels of information, even the most expensive 'state of the art' digital cameras can only register around six million pixels.

▲ A big market for hard copy prints of digitised images is in the area of video. These print packs from ICI combine with video printers made by Mitsubishi, to produce colour prints from domestic VCRs, using sublimation dye thermal transfer. As yet, the idea hasn't really taken off because printers are still quite expensive and quality is uneven – as can be seen in newspapers when the only pictures available for a news or sporting event, are derived from television images.

In publishing, the situation was totally different. The writer had to bash out his or her story on a typewriter. This was then computer-set by someone else at a bureau or printer and returned in proof form to the layout artist. This designer then cut out the proofs into 'galleys' and pasted them in the required design, onto a layout sheet. This page design was then copied by a paste-up artist, this time using high quality bromides of the text and headline setting. The resulting 'artwork' was then photographed into order to make the film which would finally produce printing plates. Using digital technology, all this work up to the film stage, can now be done by one person on one machine – hence the desk top publishing (DTP) revolution.

For a new technology to be a worthwhile investment, it needs to enable us to do work we could not do before, at a price that will not put off our customers. In publishing the advantages were clear cut, in photography, less so.

However, since we all work in the communication business, the revolution in print and publishing affects photographers too, and may eventually demand changes in working practise. With text existing in digital form, it obviously becomes convenient for pictures to be digitised too, so that they can be combined efficiently in one system. The major stumbling block has been that photographic images contain infinitely more information than text, and therefore require more complex (and expensive) equipment to digitise them and a much larger capacity storage medium. It's easy to see why. A letter in text, say an 'A' in Times typeface, remains constant and definable, whereas a colour photograph has a vast, continuously changing range of subtle shades and hues. This has meant that until recently, the digitisation of continuous tone high quality images (ie photographs), has been restricted to very expensive digital scanners.

Image capture Digital scanners use laser technology to 'read' the complex information of a photographic image (transparency or print), transforming it into strings of digital code, which is recorded onto magnetic tape or disk. Scanners now come in a range of shapes, sizes and prices. At the basic level, an inexpensive desktop scanner can be used quite effectively for monochrome line work, but produces crude results when asked to record continuous monochrome tones, yet alone colour photographs. In fact, even the most expensive scanners cannot record all the information even on a 35mm colour transparency. But then, they don't need to. The purpose of the scanner is to produce the dot structure required for the printing plate - usually between 133 and 300 dots per inch for lithographic printing. The added convenience is that complex page lay-

outs and colour pictures can now be combined electronically at so-called 'workstations'.

Machines like scanners which translate photographic images into digital form, are sometimes referred to as 'bridge technology', since they link the two technologies. In fact quite a lot of the equipment around today fits into this hybrid category. They form a compromise by using what is best in photographic technology – high quality and convenience for example – and translating it into digital form for applications such as printing, transmission across telephone lines and storage on magnetic or optical disks. It also follows that once a photographic image has been digitised, by using a computer and the appropriate software, the information can be rearranged to form something different – either a distortion or modification of the original image, or a composite of several different images.

Electronic image capture backs are now available to fit the most popular professional cameras. This means that the photographic film stage can be omitted completely, with the

▲ Symbolising, perhaps, the dilemmas facing image makers, this personal shot by CARL LYTTLE looks as though it was digitised, but it wasn't. Lyttle did the whole thing in camera. First he photographed the assembly in black and white. Then he re-photographed certain parts in colour, placing colour cutouts on a scale black and white print. The words were projected onto the curved book. The final effect was created with the Hosemaster system by literally highlighting certain elements.

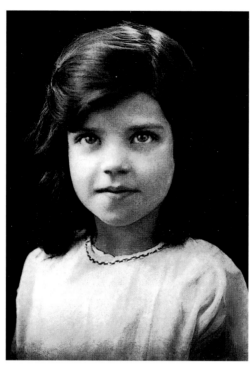

• It's not the technology itself that counts, it's what you do with it. Colab's 'Caring Memories' scheme is a good example of digital imaging used to fulfil a real demand in the market. The Coventry-based lab produced point-of-sale display material for photographers, shops and minilabs to encourage customers to bring in old photographs for restoration. These prints, often scratched or damaged, are then scanned electronically and displayed on a monitor. Creases and scratches can be 'filled in' while missing pieces can be replaced, often by copying other parts of the photograph. In some cases, people can even be moved from one photo to another. Contrast and brightness can also be improved. 'New' photographs are then produced via a dye-sublimation printer and mounted ready for framing.

camera itself translating the live image into digital form. This might sound attractive, but digital backs are not cheap, and though image resolution is getting higher and higher, you still need a good reason to use them rather than a conventional camera loaded with silver halide film. For example, in certain studio catalogue work, where savings in time and money could be made over conventional scanning for reproduction, digital backs might make sense. But for most work, we would advise a watching brief. The prices will come down and the quality will improve.

Meanwhile, if you need your pictures digitised for manipulation or composite work, you're probably better off buying a scanner or taking your photographs to a bureau, where experts will scan and manipulate them to your instructions. Remember, by sticking with silver halide photography for origination, your image quality is higher and you retain the potential for many different uses: low cost prints, high quality display

'Clients are looking for an extension to reality, and photographers can now use digital imaging to combine elements of transparencies to create new images. Digital imaging widens the spectrum by making a greater percentage of a photographer's shots workable, since a good shot can now be turned into a great shot. Photographers should not be afraid that the digital process will take away creativity – in fact it will add to it.'

Sheldon Marshall, Visual Communications Ltd.

enlargements, digital scanning for repro or manipulation, slide projection, duping and so on.

Hard copy One of the major drawbacks with digital imaging is that good hard copies are difficult and expensive to obtain. Whereas film was originally designed with photographic prints in mind, digitised images exist in a form most suited to other electronic devices such as magnetic disks, VDU screens or telephone modems. Certainly this has been the major stumbling block in any attempts by the manufacturers to conquer the lucrative amateur market. Even by modest D&P standards, the quality of hard copies just hasn't been good enough – nor has the price been suficiently low.

For the professional, this need not be a problem, although most people find the existence of some kind of hard copy, reassuring. High quality hard copies from digital images are available, though the equipment is very expensive and found mostly in the pre-press area where they are needed for proofing.

Another interesting alternative is to use colour laser copiers – expensive to buy but available at most professional labs and, for that matter, your local copy shop. Unfortunately your local shop may not have the Raster Image Processor (RIP) necessary to convert the digital information into a form the copier understands. But colour copier technology can also be useful for straight proofing from transparencies, negs or prints – indeed some photographers now use colour 'laser-prints' for their portfolios.

Finally, various types of 'photo-printers' are now available which essentially accept that photographic processes produce the best hard copies, and so they provide a means of exposing photographic paper electronically. For photographers, at the moment, these look the best bet.

Taking the plunge One of the mixed blessings of electronic systems is that they interconnect. On the one hand this means that you can plug into a whole network of appliances, such as storage and retrieval systems, scanners linked to com-

◀ TESSA TRAEGER'S 'Homage to Claude Monet' uses digital imaging in an unusual way. The original photograph uses Traeger's well known collage technique, with vegetables meticulously arranged on her studio floor and shot from above. This transparency was then scanned and the resulting image subtly manipulated to smear and smooth over certain areas and features in order to get closer to the feeling of Monet's original.

puters for image processing, modem image transmitters and so on. On the other hand, it makes it difficult to see where your job ends and someone else's begins. Or to put it another way, at what point you should stop buying equipment (hardware and software) and buy in services instead.

There's no doubt that some people have been seduced by the technology itself, so that the game becomes more important than the end product. The danger of this route is that you could get stuck with a lot of expensive, outmoded equipment that never really paid for itself. You need to ask how often and how much extra your clients are prepared to pay for digitised or manipulated images. If demand is likely to be infrequent, then surely you are better off taking the work to a bureau; in fact even if demand is high, you may still prefer to leave this end of the process to specialists who have

invested far more heavily than you could justify, in the highest quality equipment.

Finally, if you do decide to buy, don't be rushed into anything. Remember the golden rule with hardware and software: some time in the near future, maybe next month, maybe next year, it's going to be cheaper and work better.

Materials

For many years Fuji films were the choice of certain discerning professionals, or they were used for particular jobs which suited characteristics unique to Fuji materials. Now they have come of age. There's a Fuji film – transparency, colour negative, monochrome or instant – to suit every professional requirement. And the Fuji family has grown in quality as well as quantity. In fact Fuji films can now deliver results that just weren't possible before – such as the superb, neutral blacks and whites in the Fujichrome Provia test shot opposite

Silver-based films and papers still outshine digital media in terms of quality and cost – and Fuji offers a range of materials to suit every photo possibility

Material
advantage

▶ **Test shots for the new Fujichrome Provia. Notice the excellent colour saturation and gradation, set off by superbly neutral renderings of dense blacks and snowy whites, while flesh tones remain smooth and lifelike. Fujichrome Provia is available in three film speeds – ISO 100, 400 and 1600. Provia 100 – likely to be the most popular 'general purpose' commercial transparency film – sets new standards in granularity and sharpness.**

Over the past few years the Fuji family of sensitised materials has grown bigger and better. There's now a Fuji film – colour negative, colour transparency, black and white or instant – to meet the demands of any commercial application. And if you handle your own processing and printing, Fuji offers an equally wide choice of materials to finish the job, including internegative and duplicating film, colour negative and colour reversal papers, display transparency and all the necessary chemicals.

Fujichrome transparency
• Fujichrome Provia (ISO 100, 400 and 1600 daylight balanced) is the latest addition to Fuji's professional transparency line-up.

Provia is the result of extensive feedback from commercial, advertising and fashion photographers, telling Fuji what they want from a transparency film. As well as optimum colour

▶ Test shot on Fujicolor Reala 120 film by KEITH THOMSON. With Reala, colour rendering is enhanced by the addition of a fourth, cyan layer in the emulsion, giving a richness and subtlety of colour, closely matching the interpretation of the human eye. As a result, soft, pastel flesh tones are held, while strong, saturated colours remain bright.

balance, granularity and sharpness, the new emulsion gives good 'greyscale neutrality', rendering greys and whites with fidelity, while retaining colour accuracy. It also offers excellent push-pull characteristics and has been designed for flexibility in processing. All three versions are available in 35mm, with Provia 100 also available in 120, 220 and sheet sizes, and the 400 version in 120.

• Fujichrome Velvia (ISO 50, daylight) offers exceptionally sharp, fine grained images, ideal for fashion and advertising work. Its 17-layer emulsion structure gives vivid colour reproduction, rich skin tones and a subtle range of tones and hues. Available in all formats from 35mm to 8x10in sheet film.

• Fujichrome RTP (improved type, ISO 64, tungsten balanced) is the ideal film for studio photographers who prefer tungsten lighting. Grain texture is very fine and sharpness excellent, while enhanced colour rendering will suit most types of product and general commercial photography. It's also ideal for flat art copying. Extended reciprocity characteristics result in virtually no speed loss or colour-balance changes for long exposures (up to around 32 seconds). Colour characteristics are an excellent match for print reproduction requirements. Available in 35mm, 120 and sheet film sizes.

• Provia 100 (ISO 100, daylight) Fine grain, natural colour and neutral greyscale rendition and excellent sharpness combine to give consistently high quality results. Provia 100 is ideally suited to colour-scanner reproduction. Available in all sizes from 35mm to 8x10in sheet film.

• Provia 400 (ISO 400, daylight) is a high speed film which retains fine grain, sharpness and warm, lifelike colour characteristics. This versatile product can be push processed up to two stops, and despite its daylight balance, performs well under artificial lighting conditions. Available in 35mm and 120 formats only.

• Provia 1600 (ISO 1600, daylight) offers excellent colour rendition with the ultra-high-speed characteristics needed for action and low light photography. RSP has been colour matched for print reproduction. Available in 35mm only.

Duplicating film
• CDU (tungsten balanced) is a coupler-incorporated type colour reversal material designed to provide tungsten light exposed duplicate transparencies. This E-6 compatible film offers ideal graduation for faithful colour reproduction and good highlight-to-shadow grey balance. Available in 35mm, 70mm and sheet sizes.

Fujicolor negative
• Fujicolor Super G (ISO 100, 200, 400 and 800, daylight) films are ideally suited to action pho-

tography under all conditions. They set new standards in sharpness, fine grain and colour saturation. Available in 35mm – including 20-roll packs – Super G 100 and 400 are also available in 120.

• Fujicolor Professional NHG (ISO 400, daylight) is a high-speed print film designed for photographing people. NHG produces smooth, sharp highlights, snowy whites and dense blacks, with excellent skin tones. It also performs well across a wide range of lighting conditions. Available in 35mm and 120 only.

• Fujicolor NPS (ISO 160, daylight) is the most recent addition to Fuji's professional colour negative range. Building on the success of Fujicolor NSP, it benefits from the latest advances in technology to give more natural skin tones, improved sharpness and granularity and fine detail with a natural softness ideal for portraiture and people pictures in general. Highlight and shadow detail are excellent, with good neutrality and highly forgiving exposure latitude. Available in 35mm, 120, 220 and sheet sizes.

• Fujicolor NPL (ISO 160, tungsten balanced) offers similar characteristics to NPS but is designed for artificially lit interiors. Available in 120 and sheet sizes only.

• Fujicolor Reala (ISO 100, daylight) uses precision chemistry to capture all the subtle tonal gradations perceived by the human eye. The result is true-to-life images of exceptionally fine grain, which yield outstanding enlargements. Available in 35mm and 120 only.

Neopan black and white negative
• Neopan 400 Professional (ISO 400) is a versatile monochrome material with outstandingly fine grain, high resolution, wide exposure latitude and excellent tonal gradation from shadows to highlight detail. Development is process-friendly in a variety of chemicals and its smooth, flexible finish was designed for use with motor-drives. Available in 35mm and 120 sizes only.

• Neopan 1600 Professional (ISO 1600) is an ultra-high-speed monochrome film with excellent push/pull characteristics. Its grain structure, definition and image texture, are unrivalled in the ISO 400-1600 range. Available in 35mm only.

Additional film products
• Fuji Professional Instant FP100C (ISO 100) delivers peel-apart test images of outstanding colour accuracy and clarity. With its speed matched to the popular Fujichrome RDP, Fuji's own instant film has proved a hit with professionals since its launch in 1992. Available in packs of 10 in two sizes: 3.25 x 4.25in (gloss or silk finish) and 4 x 5in (gloss only).

• Fujichrome Quickload offers the convenience of 20-sheet packs designed for use with

▲ This test shot on Fujicolor Professional NHG shows remarkable sharpness and granularity for a high speed (ISO 400) colour negative film. It also demonstrates how well NHG, in common with most Fuji materials, handles the mixed lighting conditions often found on interior location jobs.

Polaroid film holders. It's available with either Fujichrome Velvia (ISO 50) or Fujichrome Provia RDPII (ISO 100).

• Fujicolor Internegative IT-N (new version) delivers superior colour negatives (and hence superb prints) from Fujichrome transparencies and other reversal films. Lifelike colour, ultra-fine grain and excellent sharpness, are combined with newly enhanced, realistic gradation and improved handling characteristics, to give significantly improved finished prints.

IT-N is available in 35mm (long roll), 4x5in and 8x10in sheet sizes.

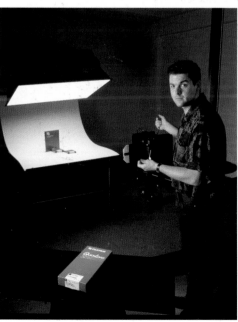

▲ Fuji's professional instant peel-apart material – FP100C – delivers such clarity and accuracy of colour, that some photographers use it to originate images, though its primary function is for testing lighting, exposure, composition and colour balance.

◄ Fujichrome Quickload is popular with photographers wanting the convenience of 20-shot packs designed for use in film holders. Quickload is available with either Fujichrome Velvia (ISO 50) or Fujichrome Provia RDPII (ISO 100).

As a commercial photographer, you are judged not by the amount of work you put into a job, but by the final image you present to the client. So first-class processing, printing and presentation are vital to your success. Should you trust this important work to an outside laboratory, or retain control by handling it yourself? In-house processing – especially in colour – can mean a heavy investment: the decision should be based on strict, business criteria

Processing

▶ **CMB Visual Communications is a large company in Swindon whose business covers colour processing and printing, computer graphics, exhibition display work, location and studio photography. Equipped to produce a full range of products up to the large display prints shown here, the colour lab is much more than a service department. In fact it could be regarded as CMB's core business.**

Home or away?

Because you spend so much on processing, you might be tempted to bring it in house – but there are many more important factors that you should take into account

In his book on printing, Ansel Adams compared the negative to a musical score: like the composer, the photographer has made his composition, now it awaits the concert performance. This might seem a grandiose way of thinking about commercial processing and printing, but it puts the emphasis in the right place. All the effort of setting up and taking a photograph, can be severely undermined by poor processing and printing.

Perhaps part of the problem has been the parting of ways between picture taking and processing. In the early days, the idea of photography implied taking the image the whole way through to the final print. On location, pioneers such as the Victorian war photographer Roger Fenton, often took their darkrooms with them in the form of covered wagons. You didn't slip out to the local lab to have a few prints done!

To an extent, the link still remains with black and white photography. We no longer coat our own glass plates with home-brewed emulsions, but many photographers still enjoy controlling in the darkroom the final appearance of the images they have made. Such involvement can also lead to further refinements such as print toning and the rediscovery of old processes such as gum bichromate or platinum printing. In fact this

  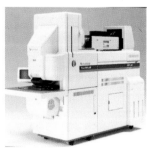

• Minilabs like these from Fuji, greatly simplify the business of processing and printing. The main advantages of compact models – speed and convenience – are particularly suited to general D&P work, but some larger machines have sufficient versatility to suit a busy commercial studio. The Fuji SFA-252 can handle all formats from 35mm to 120 (including panoramic sizes), has a built-in colour scanner with colour monitor, allows cropping and produces prints up to 12x8in.

◄ Coventry-based Colab is a good example of a modern, multi-purpose laboratory. After 25 years in the business it now runs satellite operations in Birmingham, Wolverhampton, Nottingham, Cheltenham and Cardiff. Colab's size and success depends on the fact that it caters for all sectors of the market: professional photographers, exhibition display clients and general D&P customers. At Coventry a wide range of services are covered, from giant display prints to digital imaging, from machine 'packages' to hand printing. The complexity of the operation demands constant investment in new equipment, well trained staff and persistent quality control.

▲ *Jean Lock is the 'name' printer at Visions, a small colour lab in West London. Through producing exhibition-quality prints, mainly for leading advertising and fashion photographers, she has built up such a reputation that top fashion magazines throughout the world have been placing orders. Since most of her clients shoot transparency, Lock prefers to work through internegs rather than reversal printing, because this route gives her an added degree of control and flexibility for the final print. On these pages she shows us a series of enhancements made at the printing stage. Some of the changes are quite subtle, because Lock is such a perfectionist that even the 'before' prints are better than those many labs would produce!*

▶ **For this fashion shot, RHODY SIMS wanted the sky darkened to echo the colour of the model's dress. The lighter 'straight' print is shown, left. In the finished print, Jean Lock has also lightened the model's hair slightly and darkened an obtrusive stone in the bottom right corner. Darkening skies is a fairly common request and can only be accomplished by burning in.**

◄ When Rob Brimson brought this image to Visions ('straight' print from transparency shown below left), he wanted Jean Lock to match the quality (darker background and so on) of his original test print on instant material, since the client had preferred this to the transparency. Lock's template shows the burning and dodging necessary to achieve this effect.

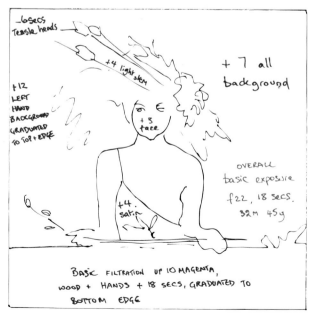

▲ The Fuji Pictrostat 200 functions rather like colour copier, though the repro technology is photographic (thermal transfer) rather than electrostatic. From original prints, transparencies or small three-dimensional objects, it produces photographic prints up to A4 size, with reduction/magnification from 50-200% available in 1% increments.

whole area gives scope for a range of subtle variations on the expected appearance of photographic prints – a genuine bonus since success in photography often depends on surprising the viewer.

With the advent of colour photography, keeping tabs on the whole image making process became rather more difficult. It's not so much that making a good colour print takes more skill – it doesn't – rather that colour processing and printing requires a bigger investment and more space, is more complicated and takes more time. So for commercial photographers the choice is simple: whether to use a specialist colour laboratory or to set up your own facility in house, usually employing or training up lab technicians to handle the work.

As with choosing the size and location of your studio, the decision to set up processing in-house should be based on strict business criteria, though in practice, such decisions usually have an emotional content. Ask photographers why they set up their own processing and they'll tell you about frustration with lab quality and service, or the wish to have greater control over their work.

But if technical quality is the only objective, then it's usually easier to achieve this through an outside laboratory. Most labs have the equipment, the materials, the controls and the staff to produce high quality work. If you feel that you are not getting the right service, then either complain or move. Unfortunately a few labs still tend to cater for the expectations of their clients – in other words what they feel they can get away with – so if no one complains, they have no incentive to improve. It also has to be said that photographers are usually reluctant to take any of the blame for poor quality results – when sometimes the fault lies with inaccurate exposure, lack of contrast control or uneven lighting. So before taking the big step of setting up your own processing, it's worth talking things through with lab staff. Once the lab understands your requirements, it should have no trouble in providing you with quality standards at least equal to what you could achieve yourself.

Like a big studio, in-house processing is a heavy commitment and a constant overhead. So before proceeding, you need to make a careful analysis of existing work. The first thing to consider is what type of photography you do and how it is presented. For example, if you work mainly for clients in the advertising or fashion fields, then you'll probably be supplying mostly transparencies. The main bonuses of in-house film processing – such as E-6 for transparencies – are convenience and speed of turnaround, the financial advantages are negligible. So, if an E-6 line is something you can afford and would offer a better service to your clients, then go for it. But if you are just starting

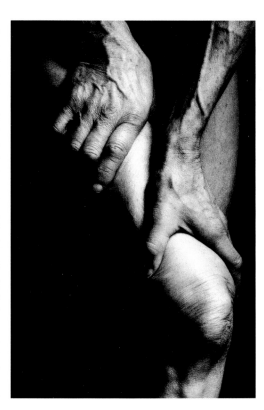

to build your business and don't want the extra hassle, then it's better to stick with a good lab.

The situation may be very different with a general commercial studio. Look at what you sell, both now and, if possible, estimate what future demand is likely to be. The key area is print sales: if you supply long print runs (eg for PR or sales use) or large prints for display and exhibition purposes, then in-house processing is well worth considering. In fact, with careful planning and development, it could become the cornerstone of your business. In the past, some studios have been so successful at this side of the business, that they gave up photography completely and became commercial laboratories.

So let's suppose that your business meets these criteria and that the possibility of in-house processing looks worth exploring. Here are some factors to consider:

Financial Analyse you lab bills for the year. From this you should be able to work out unit costs for various sizes of print. Most manufacturers of processing and printing equipment, will supply unit costs for certain minimum throughputs, so that you can make meaningful comparisons. Treat these conservatively because they probably don't allow for staff costs and wastage. If the figures still look interesting, then you need to decide, perhaps with your bank manager, what level of investment you can afford.

Space It could be said that this factor should

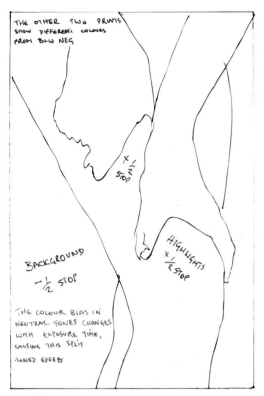

Handwritten annotations on sketch:
THE OTHER TWO PRINTS SHOW DIFFERENT COLOURS FROM B/W NEG

× ½ STOP

HIGHLIGHTS × ½ STOP

BACKGROUND − ½ STOP

THE COLOUR BIAS IN NEUTRAL TONES CHANGES WITH EXPOSURE TIME, CAUSING THIS SPLIT-TONED EFFECT

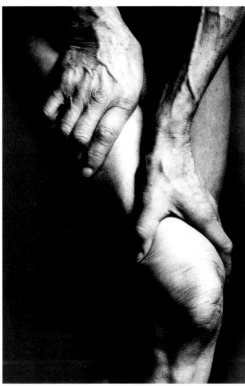

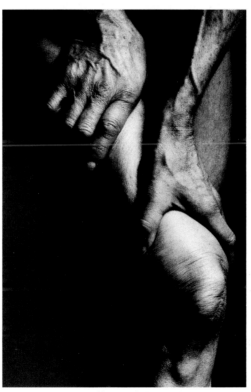

◄ In these prints from a black and white negative by STEPHEN COLOVER, JEAN LOCK shows how the colour bias in neutral tones changes with exposure time, causing a split-toned effect.

have come first, because without sufficient space for colour printing, processing, mixing chemicals, drying and finishing, then the whole idea is a non-starter. Visit one or two of your colleagues and study their processing set-ups. Now consider what room you have available in your own premises, allowing if possible, for future expansion.

Staff & Equipment The type of equipment you choose relates closely to what staff you have available or are prepared to hire. For example, automatic equipment (eg machine printers) is more expensive but takes less skill to operate – so it should not be difficult to train existing staff to take on the extra responsibility. Hand printing, on the other hand, takes greater skill, so an experienced colour technician may be needed. When looking for staff, remember that a good lab technician needs common sense, a level head and a methodical approach. Would-be photographers seldom make the best recruits because they tend to be quickly frustrated by the work.

Obviously your choice of equipment will also relate to what the bulk of your work is liable to be. For example if the main demand is for small prints, say 5x7 or 10x8-inch, with only the occasional request for large display prints, then it would be foolish to buy a 24-inch processor. Bigger print jobs can be put out to your local lab.

Potential growth As with any business venture, it can't all be worked out precisely on paper. Through talking to clients, both existing and potential, you'll need to get a feeling for what future demand is likely to be. Remember that in the past, seeing yourself principally as a photographer, you may have been reluctant to push the idea of long print runs or display prints. Once you can supply these services directly, it could be a different story.

Photographers' Profiles

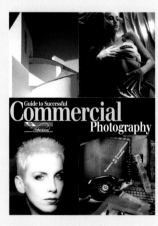

• Cover photographs, clockwise from top left: IAN McKINNELL, SANDERS NICOLSON; CARL LYTTLE; SANDERS NICOLSON. All photographs © the photographer.

The author and publishers offer sincere thanks to the Professional Photographic Division of Fuji Photo Film Ltd, for their support and encouragement, and to the following professionals, whose willingness to contribute their time, business ideas, technical secrets, inspiration and examples of their work, made this book possible.

ACE PHOTO AGENCY is one of Britain's leading photo libraries, carrying a wide range of colour transparencies across most of the mainstream subject areas: people, lifestyles, business, industry, leisure, travel, arts, abstracts, textures and so on. Digital image storage and transmission are seen by the company as the next logical progression. *Contact: 071-495 6100*

GRAHAME AUSTIN (Kitchenham) is a 'GP' photographer based in Bournemouth, who has made aerial photography, on a local basis, an important part of his business. He finds it lifts the profile of his studio too. *Contact: 0202-513 387*

MARTIN BECKETT is an advertising/editorial photographer who has tended to specialise in people pictures, including some compelling editorial portraits, but is equally at home with general location work. *Contact: 0374-161 886*

STEVE BICKNELL specialises in industrial, corporate and general commercial work. On location and in the studio, his work is noted for its powerful lighting and strong compositional sense. *Contact: 0403-784 311*

NORMAN CHILDS has shifted from purely industrial to corporate and architectural work (mostly interiors). His elegant style is backed by a thorough understanding of lighting techniques. *Contact: 0442-259 265*

IAN COATES is one of Britain's leading wedding and portrait photographers, who is equally at home in the corporate world of executive portraiture. Although a master of technique, he maintains that in portraiture, expression is what matters most. *Contact: 0625-527 877*

PETER DAZELEY is an advertising photographer whose speciality is realising the wild imaginings of art directors. Through a combination of excellent photographic technique and digital image manipulation, he usually finds the solution. *Contact: 071-736 3171*

MIKE HEMSLEY (Walter Gardiner Photography) brings to industrial/commercial photography, a fine understanding of lighting and composition. For composite work, he prefers the rostrum to the digital editing suite and says his clients appreciate the lower bills too. *Contact: 0903-200 528*

CHRISTOPHER JOYCE has been in the vanguard of advertising photography for over three decades. He finds that personal, black and white 35mm work helps to maintain his enthusiasm – recently it's been earning him money too. *Contact: 071-287 6118*

JON LIPPET specialises mainly in studio still life work: pack shots, drinks, jewellry and other artefacts. In his spare time he literally rises above it all as a keen hot air balloonist. *Contact: 071-748 0871*

JEAN LOCK (Visions) is one of Britain's most respected colour printers. She is an obsessive perfectionist who will often spend half the night adjusting and reprinting a single exhibition print. *Contact: 071-748 0871*

PETER LOWRY is a talented GP photographer who does fine work in many fields: commercial, industrial, corporate, weddings, portraits and architectural. Specialising might have earned him more, but he enjoys the variety. *Contact: 0373-461 779*

CARL LYTTLE learned the ropes assisting for Chris Joyce, but is now a respected advertising photographer in his own right. Though happy to use digital techniques commercially, in his personal work, he is a keen explorer of old colour printing methods. *Contact: 071-287 0884*

TOM MACKIE was born an American but has settled in the UK where he specialises in large format landscape work, mainly for the calendar market. Best sellers, he says, are winter studies and pictures with water reflections. *Contact: 0850 848911*

DANNY MADDOCKS valiantly upholds the visual traditions of powerful industrial photography, though he recognises that, as corporate imagery goes, these days VDU screens tend to be more popular than steel mills. *Contact: 091-268 8000*

IAN MCKINNELL specialises in architectural photography for both editorial and corporate clients. For exterior work, he says, it's mostly about the weather – the light is everything. *Contact: 071-631 3017*

JULIAN NIEMAN takes pictures to illustrate magazine features on interesting houses and buildings. Under pressure to 'get more shots done in a day', he tends to favour small format equipment. *Contact: 081-883 1576*

SANDERS NICOLSON has devoted most of his successful advertising career to photographing people, whether beauty, fashion, portrait or 'lifestyle'. Although keen to make believable pictures, he is also fascinated by representation – the way an image communicates. *Contact: 071-739 6987*

PAUL PROCTOR does around 400 hours of flying time a year, as principal aerial photographer for Chorley and Handford. Whether you need a shot of Piccadilly Circus, an archaeological site or a nuclear power station, it's either in his library or he'll get up there and shoot it. *Contact: 081-669 4900*

BILL PRUDOM is a GP commercial photographer based in Manchester, who concentrates mainly on PR work. He business, he says, is based on service and fast turnaround: 'Nobody wants to wait more than 24-hours for a job.' *Contact: 061-320 3089*

MICHAEL ST MAUR SHEIL specialises in corporate photography – assignments take him all over the world. He travels light and dislikes stage management, preferring a photojournalistic approach – often with striking results. 'I photograph what I see,' he says. *Contact: 036787 276*

TESSA TRAEGER photographs perishable natural forms: vegetables, fruit, flowers, food. Her sensitivity to shape, texture and colour is second to none. *Contact: 071-352 3641*

PAUL WEBSTER is a food photographer who specialises in ice cream – always the real thing, never fake material. The secret, he says, is to work quickly and use a good stylist. *Contact: 081-749 0264*

The author, **CHRISTOPHER WORDSWORTH**, studied photography in the early 1970s at Guildford under Walter Nurnberg, and after a short spell as a commercial studio photographer, has been writing about it ever since. He has edited several photographic magazines and is the author of Fuji Professional Wedding and Portrait Photography (published by the British Journal of Photography, first edition 1991, revised edition 1993). *Contact: 0985 847709*

Index

Main chapter headings are shown in bold, photographers in italics.

USEFUL CONTACTS

**Association of Photographers
(formerly AFAEP)**
9-10 Domingo Street, London
EC1 OTA Tel: 071-608 1441

**British Association of Picture
Libraries and Agencies
(BAPLA)**
13 Woodberry Crescent, London
N10 1PJ Tel: 081-444 7913

**British Institute of
Professional Photography
(BIPP)**
Talbot House, Amwell End, Ware,
Herts SG12 9HN
Tel: 0920-464011

**British Journal of
Photography**
Timothy Benn Publishing Ltd,
186-187 Temple Chambers,
Temple Avenue, London EC4Y
0DB Tel: 071-583 3030

Fuji Photo Film (UK) Ltd
Fuji Film House, 125 Finchley
Road, London NW3 6JH
Tel: 071-586 5900

**Master Photographers
Association**
Hallmark House, 97 East Street,
Epsom, Surrey KT17 1EA
Tel: 0372-726123

Royal Photographic Society
The Octagon, Milsom Street, Bath
BA11 1DN Tel: 0225-462841